The Students' Library
PRELUDE TO EAST AFRICAN HISTORY

Prelude to East African History

a collection of papers given at the First East
African Vacation School in Pre-European
African History and Archaeology in
December 1962

Edited by
MERRICK POSNANSKY

*with a preface by the President of the British
Institute of History and Archaeology in
East Africa*

L. P. Kirwan

LONDON

Oxford University Press

IBADAN · NAIROBI

1966

Oxford University Press, Ely House, London W.1

GLASGOW NEW YORK TORONTO MELBOURNE WELLINGTON
CAPE TOWN SALISBURY IBADAN NAIROBI LUSAKA ADDIS ABABA
BOMBAY CALCUTTA MADRAS KARACHI LAHORE DACCA
KUALA LUMPUR HONG KONG

PRINTED IN GREAT BRITAIN
BY LATIMER TREND AND CO LTD
PLYMOUTH

Preface

This book is the fruit of a week's Vacation Course held at Makerere University College, Uganda, in 1962 by the British Institute of History and Archaeology in East Africa. Its editor, then the Institute's Assistant Director, is now Director of African Studies at Makerere. The object of the Course, attended not only by residents in Uganda but by students from many parts of East and Central Africa, was to provide an introduction and a background to the study of the pre-European history and archaeology of East Africa. The papers published here therefore range in date from the Stone Age down to the early mediaeval city ports on the coast which traded with the interior and linked East Africa with Arabia and Persia, India and China; and on to the first coastal settlements of the Portuguese. Between these extremes lie the twelve centuries or more of East Africa's Iron Age, now being explored by means of the most modern archaeological techniques. From the point of view of contemporary East Africa this is in many respects the most important period for it was then that the foundations of modern tribal society were being laid.

The British Institute which sponsored these lectures and discussions was founded in 1959 under the auspices of the British Academy which provides most of its funds. If it can be said to have had a father it is the Secretary of that Academy, the distinguished archaeologist Sir Mortimer Wheeler who foresaw the great possibilities for historical research and archaeological discovery which East Africa held, and holds, in store.

Preface

Geographically the Institute's scope includes Kenya, Tanzania and Uganda and although its headquarters are in Nairobi its field work takes place in all three countries. Primarily it is preoccupied with its own research in East African history and archaeology. But as a 'Connected Institute' of the University of East Africa, it also contributes through teaching, through training, and through the offer of studentships, to the development of higher education in East Africa.

It also has a wider role, that of stimulating an interest among non-specialists in the objective, scientific, study of East Africa's pre-European history and archaeology, not least among East Africans themselves. This will help to enable them (and others) to relate the Past to the elucidation of some of the problems of contemporary Africa. If, as I am sure that they will, the lectures published in this book can help in such respects, they will have served their purpose well.

L. P. Kirwan
President, British Institute of History and Archaeology in East Africa

Contents

Contents

Contributors

MISS RUTH C. BERGER Former research student of the British Institute of History and Archaeology in East Africa.

DR. W. W. BISHOP Lecturer in Geology, Bedford College, London, formerly curator of the Uganda Museum.

MR. H. N. CHITTICK Director of the British Institute of History and Archaeology in East Africa.

MR. GLYNN ISAAC Former Director, Kenya National Museum Centre for Prehistory and Palaeontology.

MR. JAMES KIRKMAN Warden of the coastal sites of the Royal National Parks in Kenya and curator of Fort Jesus Museum.

MR. BRYAN KIRWAN Uganda linguist.

DR. L. S. B. LEAKEY Director of the Kenya National Museum Centre for Prehistory and Palaeontology; Viking Fund Medallist, 1962.

DR. B. ALAN OGOT Chairman of History Department, University College, Nairobi.

PROFESSOR AIDAN SOUTHALL Professor of Sociology, University of Syracuse, U.S.A.

DR. JOHN E. G. SUTTON Lecturer in History, University College, Dar-es-Salaam.

DR. M. POSNANSKY (Editor) Director of African Studies at Makerere University College.

Figures

Maps

Plates

1 A Power Grip, flaking a 'chopping tool' with a hammerstone held in the right hand.*Photograph, J. R. Napier*

2 Dr. L. S. B. Leakey cutting the ligaments of an animal leg, using a flake detached in making a 'chopping tool'.

3 Dr. L. S. B. Leakey shaping a handaxe.

4 Olorgesailie—'A natural filing system of Prehistoric remains'. Stratified lake deposits, banked against the foot of Mt. Olorgesailie, have been disrupted by earth movements. Erosion now makes accessible objects which were once deeply buried. *Photograph, G. Isaac*

5 The final phases of excavating and recording a prehistoric camp site. An area, some 12 yards in diameter, is littered with stone tools and broken-up bones of animals. The baulks enclose the area first excavated by Dr. Leakey in 1942 and preserved as a public exhibition. *Photograph, G. Isaac*

6 Part of the camp floor illustrated in Plate 6, femur of *Simopithecus*, a giant baboon, now extinct, lies next to a cluster of handaxes. *Photograph, G. Isaac*

7 An erosion gully at Nsongezi, Uganda, cut through old swamp deposits, from which numerous Sangoan and Lupemban tools have been recovered. *Photograph, G. Cole*

8 Magosi, Uganda. An inselberg with two rock-shelters inhabited from Middle Stone Age times.

Acknowledgements

The help of all contributors is gratefully acknowledged both for their lectures, which formed the basis of a most successful vacation school and for their help and patience in editing their transcriptions and written contributions. Especial thanks are tendered to Neville Chittick for constant advice, valuable criticism and editorial help and to Dr. John Sutton for his assistance in running the seminar and reading proofs. For photographs I am grateful to Dr. J. R. Napier, Mr. H. N. Chittick, Dr. G. Cole, Mr. Glynn Isaac and Mr. James Kirkman; for figures VI–X to Mr. G. Nyerwanire, the original drawing on which figure X is based to Mr. P. Garlake, figure V and map 3 to Dr. John Sutton and maps 4 and 5 to Mr. H. N. Chittick. I am indebted to Mrs. Jenkins, Mrs. Marrable and John Muzoora for typing the scripts at various stages. In any book about African history the rate of new discoveries very rapidly overtakes the pace of editorial work and publication and in this case the delay has been appreciable, for which I am mostly to blame. The reader is asked to appreciate that the contributions largely date from December 1962 and to excuse the contributors for the 'dated' nature of their chapters for which they are not to blame.

MERRICK POSNANSKY

Los Angeles
April 1966

Introduction

It is an essentially human characteristic to be conscious of oneself and amongst virtually all peoples stories of creation occur, and every tribe seeks to know its origin. Very often the origins are enshrouded in myth and legend. History and archaeology provide means to establish facts about the past and to interpret them in as true a way as possible. Before the research work began it was assumed that Africa had no past and these myths and legends were ignored. The archaeologists have now for over fifty years shown that Africa has a past and have led the way to its appraisal by using the techniques of the prehistorian and the anthropologist, particularly for the more recent past which perhaps has the more immediate interest. The myths and legends are being critically studied and a history is emerging from them.

For many years the work in Africa has been conducted by isolated workers and under great difficulties and little attempt has been made to communicate the results of the work by mass media to the public of Africa. Nevertheless the work has been vital and has helped to build up a framework of dates and of key sites on which we can now erect our story.

What are the achievements in the field of archaeology and history in Africa? What are the scholars finding out? These are the questions asked of us and in the last few years the cumulative results of research throughout the Continent have been impressive.

The results have been the fruit of co-operation by scholars from different disciplines and different countries. As early as 1947 the prehistorians under the inspiring leadership of Dr. Leakey came together in a Pan-African Conference held in Nairobi and since that time periodic conferences of both historians and prehistorians have been held.

During those past eighteen years it is fair to say that the most important contribution of the archaeologists to human knowledge has been the confirmation by repeated new discoveries that Africa was the original homeland of Mankind. Not only have the remains of fossil hominids been found but also of the primate ancestors of those hominids. From Kenya in the late 1940's came the finds of *Proconsul*, one of the first apes to develop as an unspecialized primate adept at running on the plains and swinging in the trees. These discoveries from Miocene localities, principally from the Kavirondo area of Kenya, dating back to twenty or twenty-five million years ago have been paralleled in the last two or three years by new finds of the *genus Proconsul* from Karamoja in Uganda, primarily by Dr. Bishop of the Uganda Museum, which have extended our knowledge of the territorial range and the ecology of these simian ancestors. More recently at Fort Ternan in Kenya Dr. Leakey has found, in what are believed to be Pliocene beds some fourteen million years old, a primate between *Proconsul* and the australopithecenes, from whom man himself may have derived, and which he has provisionally called *Kenyapithecus wickeri*. In South Africa large numbers of australopithecines have been found at different localities which have given us a good idea of the creature, which we can say broke the 'human barrier' about a million and a half years ago and changed from being a scavenger to a hunter living in groups and transmitting his acquired intelligence to his young. But again, since 1959 interest has focused on East Africa with the finding by Dr. Leakey, at Olduvai gorge in the Serengeti plain of Tanzania, of no less than three superimposed sets of fossil hominid remains. These help us to visualize more clearly the hunting habits of early man and to carry the story of his physical and cultural evolution onwards to the time when he was recognizably human and making his tools in a consistently regular pattern ready to spread the first human cultures into Europe and Asia.

It is important to realize the wealth and widespread nature of these fossil remains compared to the small amount of research that has been undertaken in Africa and to note the clear fact that in Africa the whole succession of tools exists from the earliest occasional attempts at stone-flaking some million and a half years ago to the elaborate handaxes of around quarter of a million years ago.

In Asia and Europe on the other hand the first tools are those self-same later fully evolved handaxes.

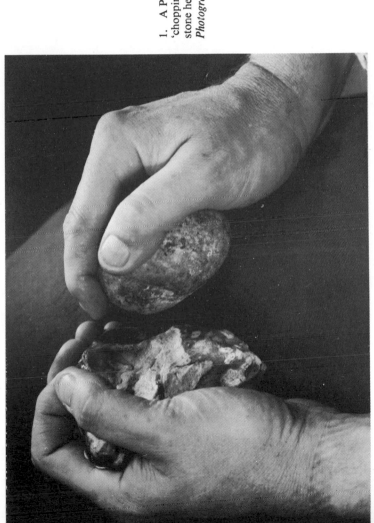

1. A Power Grip. Flaking a 'chopping tool' with a hammer-stone held in the right hand. *Photograph: J. R. Napier.*

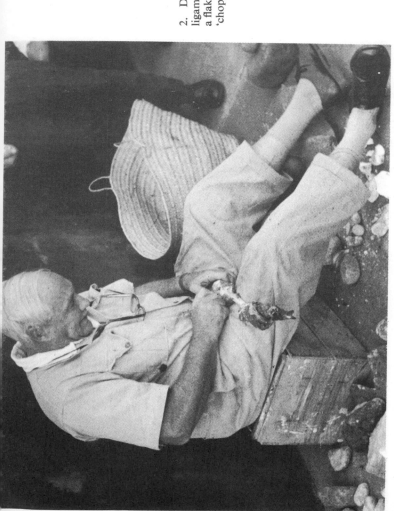

2. Dr. L. S. B. Leakey cutting the ligaments of an animal leg using a flake detached in making a 'chopping tool'.

3. Dr. L. S. B. Leakey shaping a handaxe.

4. *Left*: Olorgesailie—'A natural filing system of Prehistoric remains'. Stratified lake deposits, banked against the foot of Mt. Olorgesailie, have been disrupted by earth movements. Erosion now makes accessible objects which were once deeply buried.
Photograph: G. Isaac.

5. *Below*: The final phases of excavating and recording a pre-historic camp site. An area, some 12 yards in diameter, is littered with stone tools and broken-up bones of animals. The baulks enclose the area first excavated by Dr. Leakey in 1942 and preserved as a public exhibition.
Photograph: G. Isaac.

6. *Left:* Part of the camp floor illustrated in plate 5: femur of *Simopithecus*, a giant baboon, now extinct, lies next to a cluster of handaxes.
Photograph: G. Isaac.

7. *Below:* An erosion gully at Nsongezi, Uganda, cut through old swamp deposits, from which numerous Sangoan and Lupemban tools have been recovered.
Photograph: G. Cole.

8. Magosi, Uganda. An inselberg with two rockshelters inhabited from Middle Stone Age times. The two arrows at the top point to the shelters while the arrow at the left shows the level.

9. A rock gong on Lolui Island in Lake Victoria. Striking areas are marked by arrows.

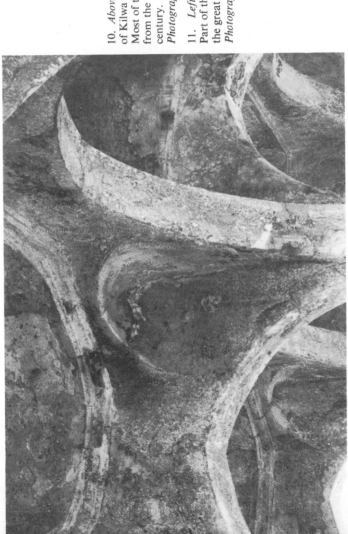

10. *Above*: The Great Mosque of Kilwa from south-west. Most of the visible parts are from the early fifteenth century.
Photograph: H. M. Chittick.

11. *Left*: Kilwa Kisiwani. Part of the domed interior of the great Mosque.
Photograph: H. N. Chittick.

12. Pillar tomb at Kaole, fourteenth–fifteenth century. The pillar is 17·5 metres high: recesses for the porcelain bowls with which it was decorated can be seen. *Photograph: H. N. Chittick.*

13. Façade of Palace at Gedi.
Fifteenth century.
Photograph: J. Kirkman.

14. Great Mosque, Ungwana (Kipini) Kenya. Verandah and tombs from north-east, fifteenth century.
Photograph: J. Kirkman.

16. Blue and white Persian bowl set in masonry to serve as a wall decoration. Probably fifteenth century; excavated at Kilwa. Diameter 15·5 cm.

Photograph: H. N. Chittick.

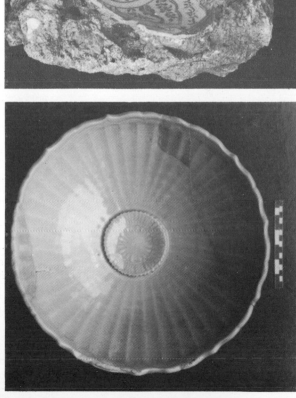

15. Chinese celadon dish, fifteenth century, from Ngomeni north of Malindi, Kenya showing typical ripple fluting.

Photograph: J. Kirkman.

17. Part of the ditch at Bigo, Uganda after clearance. Six and a half miles of ditches, often far deeper comprise this fifteenth–century capital of Western Uganda.

18. Post holes of a seventeenth–century palace at Bweyorere, Ankole, discovered with the help of oral traditions.

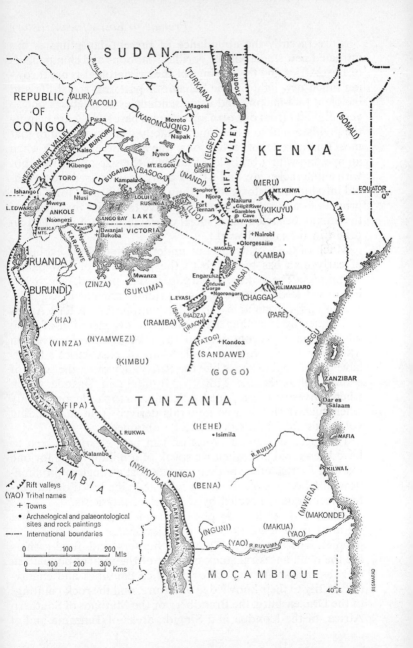

More recently the abundance of present-day primates has attracted new studies of the gorillas, baboons and chimpanzees of East Africa and the findings of the primatologists are throwing much new light on the behaviour patterns, social life and incipient tool-making and using tendencies of creatures not so very different from our own ancestors. These studies are helping the prehistorians to assess anew exactly what happened in that most fundamental of revolutions, 'the human revolution', when an apeman with a brain less than half the size of our own but with a nutcracker jaw and a thick bony head crossed the threshold into human history. More than just the physical form of the primate family was inherited; we have to realize that many of the human behavioural or social characteristics of man had an origin in the animal world.

Much of the advance in our understanding of the evolution of early man has been due to the perfection of new dating techniques. The potassium–argon dating method, which has been used to date the new fossil primate remains in Uganda, Kenya and Tanzania, is particularly applicable in East Africa as it dates by assessing the radioactive degeneration of fresh volcanic minerals contained in the lake or other deposits in which the fossils are contained. Many of East Africa's fossils have been found in zones like the Rift Valley or on the edges of extinct volcanoes like Moroto Mountain in Uganda which when active contributed fresh volcanic ash to the deposits. Only when such fresh volcanic minerals derived from surrounding volcanoes are found can a date be obtained.

The speed of human evolution can now clearly be seen to have been rapid and when we speak of a million years for one fossil or fourteen for another it is not just a rough approximation based on guesswork but a reliable guide based on laboratory techniques perfected by the nuclear-physicists.

Africa lost her leading position some 50,000 years ago but we must not underestimate the achievements of her stone-age peoples. These remarkably virile hunters and food-gathers are the main ancestral stock of most of the present population of sub-Saharan Africa. All over Africa paintings and engravings testify to their knowledge of nature, and the rock paintings of the Drakensburg, the Brandberg or the Matopos of Southern Africa, of the Kondoa and Singida areas of Tanzania and of

the Hoggar and the Tassili ranges of the Sahara are the equal
of any rock paintings in the world. In Tanzania alone the
sites with naturalistic art are numbered in hundreds yet the
fullness of Africa's prehistoric art, except in South Africa, still
remains to be revealed as each year new discoveries are made.

It was once assumed that agriculture was a very recent introduction into Africa from the near East. In recent years intensive research by the palaeobotanists has begun to suggest that
parts of Africa were not as late in their shift to a food-producing economy as had been thought. Work on the bananas in
Africa has shown that many new varieties have originated in
the upland areas of East Africa and the classification of the
types indicates that they came from Indonesia before the spread
of the Arab Indian Ocean trade towards the end of the first
millennium A.D. which brought with it a different variety still.
Certain of the millets seem to have originated either in Ethiopia
or in West Africa and it has been seriously proposed that cotton
may be Africa's gift to Asia. Though it is generally assumed
that the idea of agriculture spread to Africa about six to seven
thousand years ago it is possible that the cultivation of yams
and certain other forest crops had an indigenous 'vegecultural'
origin. New discoveries in the Sahara, of pottery types like that
of the 'dotted wavy line' ware, indicate the contact that existed
between the Middle Nile and the Chad region as early as
3000 B.C. Historians are actively speculating on the scale of the
contribution of the cultures of Nubia, from the Meroitic culture
of the last millennium B.C. to the fall of Christian Nubia, not
only in technological developments such as iron working but
also in statecraft and religion.

In the last few years linguists have also entered the fray and
have attempted to bring some order to the linguistic map of
Africa and to work out the way Africa has been peopled. Gone
are the old concepts of the Hamites of the Horn mixing with
Nilotics from the Sudan to provide Nilo-hamites; gone is the
idea that what was advanced in Africa was due to successive
inoculations of this higher culture into a backward Negro
world. In their place there has been fresh thinking on the
origins of the Bantu-speaking peoples and their dispersal. The
dispersal of the Bantu by all accounts was explosive, with small
groups rapidly filling a comparatively empty Southern Africa

but from where they came there is some doubt; some authorities suggest the Cameroons–Nigerian borderland and one, the Zambezi–Congo watershed.

New dates obtained by radio–carbon dating in the Rhodesias show that there the Iron Age began some 2,000 years ago, rather earlier than had once been envisaged and not so long after the spread of iron to many parts of Western Europe.

The anatomists are also adding to the picture. New techniques of blood grouping, detailed studies of individual bone forms, biochemical tests of skin and other tissues and advances in genetics are all suggesting the inescapable fact that the Negroes originated in Africa from the Stone Age ancestral hunting and food-gathering stock. The Bushman is as specialized a variant of that stock as the Negro. But these anatomical and linguistic studies are only at a beginning. Only small samples of people have been studied and the results are proof of the need for co-operation between different disciplines.

By the end of the first millennium B.C. in Nigeria the first vigorous culture to be characterized by powerful naturalistic modelling was flourishing, that of Nok. The Nok culture, discovered first by the accidental finding of a terracotta head in tin-mining operations, is now seen to have been no isolated culture but the precursor of one of the most outstanding art traditions of the world. Repeatedly, new excavations, often in sacred groves but quite frequently in peoples' back gardens, have yielded impressive bronze figures, terracotta heads and carved stone stools. The apogee of the art was reached at Ife, south of the great kingdoms of Bornu, Ghana, Mali and Songhai, at a time when in Western Europe the Renaissance had still not provided the masterpieces of Italy, which finally began the cultural re-ascendance of Europe. At Igbo, near Onitsha in the Eastern Region, magnificent brass bowls and a treasure of figures and decorated brass calabashes, all made by *cire perdue* techniques, give some indication of the skill of the Nigerian craftsmen, who were contemporaries of the Tudors, and the munificence of even local rulers.

These rulers had contact with Muslim, but nevertheless African princes to the north and one of the important new discoveries from Africa has been the amount of contact that existed in Pre-European times.

Not all the discovery is in the hands of the archaeologists. In West Africa history is being written from unread Moorish sources; in East Africa Arabic and Swahili texts in Arabic script from the eighteenth century, many containing traditions of the Medieval period, are throwing valuable light on the trade of the Indian Ocean and on the life of the miscalled 'lost' towns of the East African Coast. The kings of Mali were visitors to Mecca in the fourteenth century where they impressed by their wealth. The Arab world was wide and alive and many of our earliest sources on Southern Africa are due to intrepid travellers like Ibn Battuta from North Africa, who in the fourteenth century made missions both to the West African kingdoms and to the East African towns. This was an era when African gold was important to the Arab world which stretched into Southern Europe and the countries of the Indian Ocean seaboard. This was a world which declined as Europe expanded to open up new sources of American gold and to extend its mercantile adventurism round Africa to the Indian Ocean.

Cities, it is true, flourished only in West Africa and on the Eastern African seaboard; but in the Rhodesias, one of the sources of the gold of the Indian Ocean trade, the effects of overseas contact were strongly felt. Zimbabwe with its thirty-foot-high dry stone-walled enclosure and mighty 'acropolis' dating back to the first millennium A.D. of the Christian era was no isolated phenomenon of Bantu achievement. The surveys of the Rhodesian Historical Monuments Commission, have listed several hundred ruins where stone houses and enclosures existed. In addition, the ethnohistorians have related what was happening at these Bantu ruins, to the story of the Bantu peopling of the Rhodesias.

But what of the heart of Africa, are we finding out anything new? Our present societies and tribal groupings owe little to these trade movements but slowly the picture begins to take some shape as the traditions of the people of Africa are closely studied. For long, the traditions of illiterate tribes were ignored, the search was for the exotic and the spectacular, but now the traditions are seen as an important mine of information which must be exploited.

Africa's past is a unity in time and must be seen against a world perspective. Past movements amongst the Galla of the

Horn of Africa affected the Sudan and the folk movements of the southern Sudan were responsible for the Nilotic peopling of Uganda. The discovery of gold in America and the expansion of European maritime knowledge led to the decline both of the Saharan and the Indian Ocean trade whilst changes of taste and fashion in the Far East had their own particular effects. These are isolated examples and many more could be cited to show that Africa or East Africa cannot be considered in isolation.

The past of Africa has often been ignored because of its drabness. On the whole, Africa, apart from the isolated exceptions of Zimbabwe, Nigeria, and the East African seaboard, and the rich cemetery at Sanga in Katanga discovered on the eve of Congo's independence, was not distinguished by material splendour or by lost civilizations; too often there has been a mistaken quest for the romantic. Though the Black Continent cannot yield a Mayan or Aztec civilization, its past, just as much as its present, was a melting-pot. Tribalism is not a new phenomenon—people have been moving, settling and being dispersed for many centuries and peoples' traditions are often the best guide to these movements. We have a need to understand our past and to create a pride in the fusion of peoples that is presently taking place. The past was not uniformally exciting but it is an individual past which needs interpreting.

On the whole Africa's past is not easy to interpret. So much of it is unevenly lit. Some areas have been visited by literate people for thousands of years whilst others were isolated. Africa is a difficult continent for the preservation of archaeological data. The acid soils are destructive of human remains and the depths of most soils are too shallow to retain the imprint of hut poles, that so often in temperate climes reveal the past habitations of Man. The thick vegetation hinders both access by roads, which are often non-existent, and masks the earthworks and mines which might otherwise have been revealed by aerial-photography. In some areas as in Rhodesia we can reconstruct the form of the *daga* or mud-plastered houses but in others like Uganda the mud-walls crumble into the soil and fade rapidly from memory. The Rift Valley zones of East Africa are favourable for the preservation of fossils with their inland basins, which have always held lakes and formerly attracted stone-age hunters, draining areas of alkaline volcanic, rocks. These ancient lakes like Olduvai have often been cleft by later earth-movement or drainage changes which have revealed by erosion their story of Man. Other areas such as the more stable edges of the Sahara in West Africa have not provided such ideal localities where fossilization could take place or where erosion has laid bare ancient living sites for the archaeologists to discover.

Many of the past societies of Africa have been primitive technologically, leaving little behind them but potsherds; and yet it is from the tiniest clues, often hidden beneath high vegetation, that we have to interpret the major movements of Africa like the origin of the Negro or the expansion of the Bantu-speaking peoples. This is not exciting archaeologically and we cannot have as our rewards the walls of temples, the sarcophagi or the jewellery of Ancient Egypt. East Africa away from the coast was isolated. The trade in copper and gold left it unaffected and trade goods never reached most of the interior until, at earliest, the seventeenth century. The early beads, except for those of resilient ostrich shell, have perished. Most of the time we are dealing with small migrant communities whose settlements have left no trace behind. In East Africa, even in the Kingdoms, houses were flimsy and it is only when we find impressive earthworks like Bigo in Buganda, with its six and a half miles of ditches, cut fifteen feet into the rock, can we feel that we have a site to come to grips with, yet at Bigo no house sites were found. The wooden pots and the calabashes have perished leaving behind only the broken pottery and the remains of meals of still fabled Bacwezi who had held sway over a large part of Western Region and part of Buganda. The work of the archaeologist is slow, first the building up a sequence to date sites and then the selection of major sites for excavation and finally the interpretation of the evidence using the combined skill of colleagues with zoological, anthropological and anatomical training to give specialist reports on bones, on village patterns or on past human groups.

It is possible to criticize some of our endeavours as worthless and to say that much of Africa's history did not contribute anything to the mainstream of world development but what we have to remember is that this is our past and as such it is a subject worthy of critical appraisal.

PART ONE

Human Evolution and the Stone Age

It is only by observing the human cultures of antiquity as elements in a changing ecological situation that it is possible to form a clear idea of even the economic basis of settlement. . . .

GRAHAME CLARK 1939

Africa's major contribution to the mainstream of human culture is probably Man himself. For much of human history Africa set the cultural pace and provided the principal reservoir of population.

The story of the emergence of Man is a long one and very much has depended on accidental discoveries and painstaking follow-up work. A very great deal of the information available has been obtained by one scientist, Dr. L. S. B. Leakey, who has excavated at Olduvai Gorge from 1931, and who discovered the first large assemblage of the Miocene *genus Proconsul* from Western Kenya and whose work has been associated with most of the major steps forward in the field of human palaeontology for nearly forty years.

East Africa has proved to be abundantly rich in sites of the Stone Age and each of the territories has one or more handaxe sites from which literally tens of thousands of stone tools have been excavated. The early sites, in contrast to those in Europe, include large numbers of undisturbed living floors which are invaluable in indicating the fullest possible information about the way of life of these early toolmakers. Such a site is Olorgesailie in Kenya described by Mr. Glynn Isaac. The Later Stone Age sites, though just as abundant, have been investigated rather less, but they provide ample opportunity in East Africa for local field work. Stone tools were employed by hunting and food-gathering peoples until almost the present day and the absorption of these stone-age survivors is a process which continues side by side with the developments described in the later chapters.

The emergence of Man was taking place in East Africa against a background of environmental change. Though not as widespread or dramatic as the movements of the ice-sheets in Europe, the changes were significant, particularly in the more unstable rift valley zones. East Africa's environment is so diverse at the present day and has been shaped by so many factors that it is often difficult to differentiate between the forces involved in the past. Until recently it was thought that, during the period of the Ice Age of the temperate latitudes, pluvial periods, when rainfall was more abundant, had prevailed in the tropics, and a detailed nomenclature was evolved from sites in Kenya and Uganda. Now it is realized that the situation is much more complicated.

Whatever the cause, the environment has undergone major changes and climatic fluctuations have been felt to a greater or lesser degree, though as yet it is impossible to say how many wetter phases there were or how widespread. Besides the necessity of understanding the nature of this environment, if one is to understand the cultural development of Man, these environmental changes have a certain value for chronology. The relative sequence of the Stone Age cultures depends on a stratigraphical sequence based on geological research. Elements of this sequence can be dated by 'absolute' methods such as potassium–argon determinations.

The main form of the rift valleys was developed well before the Early Pleistocene, possibly as long ago as thirty million years, though faulting with drops of more than a hundred feet was still taking place up till the end of the Upper Pleistocene period. A certain amount of volcanic activity also took place in the Pleistocene and such perfect cones as Kilimanjaro or Muhavura, on the Congo border of Uganda, date from the time of Stone Age Man at Olduvai. Certain volcanoes such as Ol Doinyo Lengai, north of the Serengeti plain of Tanzania, are still subactive, whilst the area to the north of Lake Edward, which lies partly in the Queen Elizabeth Game Park of Uganda, is covered with grey volcanic tuff thrown out of the ten-thousand-year-old Katwe explosion craters which give rise to a strange lunar landscape.

On the high mountains evidence of climatic changes, particularly of the last twenty thousand years, is apparent from the moraines left by the glaciers of once larger ice caps. These fluctuations are mirrored also in vegetational changes which are being studied by pollen-analytical means. Cores taken from upland bogs and through lake muds include the microscopic pollen grains of the prevailing vegetation and it is apparent that at one time during the Pleistocene Lake Victoria nearly dried up, particularly on the north and eastern margins and the grasslands expanded at the expense of the forests. Later there is evidence of the bamboo on the Kigezi mountains stretching down a full 2,000 feet below its present level indicating a cooler, damper period. Most unfortunately these changes cannot as yet be dated. Man himself affected the landscape and by the beginning of the Iron Age and possibly even as early as the first millennium B.C. forest clearance was beginning in a small way. Before that accidental fires would have taken their toll of some of the forest fringes. As a hunter, Man was also responsible for changes in the balance of animal populations by over-hunting some species and allowing others as a consequence to multiply. Unless Man is thought of as part of the wider ecological setting it is difficult to interpret the long period of the Stone Age.

1 The Prelude to Early Toolmakers in Uganda

In other parts of Africa, notably in the Fayum of Northern Egypt, it is possible to trace the ancestry of the Primate group to which Man belongs rather further back in time than in Uganda where the story commences in the Lower Miocene period some 20,000,000 years ago. The sites of Miocene age in Kenya from which fossil Primates have been found are already well known.[1] Rusinga island in Lake Victoria is perhaps the most famous but many others have been recorded by Dr. and Mrs. Leakey and their assistants.

In May 1957 and again in 1958 some fossil bones and teeth were found near the old volcanoes of Napak and Moroto in the Karamoja District of Uganda by an agricultural officer, Mr. Wilson. The Napak fossils proved to include a Lower Miocene rodent and an early cone-toothed elephant or Mastodon. Since 1958 a considerable amount of work has been carried out in Uganda and several new fossil sites have been found. Thus the prelude to the early toolmakers in Uganda may be said from the present evidence to have commenced in Karamoja some 20 million years ago.

The eroded volcano of Napak lies on the Teso–Karamoja border with the main fossil sites to the south-west of the former volcanic vent. The original cone stood at least 10,000 feet high and was almost twenty-five miles across at the base but it is represented now only by a series of small relict hills. The other main Miocene fossil sites in Uganda are some fifty miles away from Napak towards the north-east. They lie to the north of the much less dissected and much more mountainous former volcano of Moroto mountain.

The majority of the fossils have been preserved beneath

[1] Bishop, W. W. and Whyte, F., 1962, 'Tertiary Mammalian Faunas and Sediments in Karamoja and Kavirondo, East Africa', *Nature*, vol. 196, pp. 1283–87.

layers of volcanic ash which afterwards solidified into tuff and they represent the creatures which lived on the slopes of the active cone of the volcano about six miles from the actual vent through which the debris was ejected which built up the cone. During quiet spells in the volcano's activity, vegetation was able to clothe at least the lower slopes of the volcano and support the animals. Some sites which yield more poorly preserved specimens and which are less abundantly fossiliferous occur at the base of the old volcanic cone and rest immediately on the Basement Complex rocks which underlie the majority of the Karamoja plain. The sites of this type at Napak closely resemble those at Moroto.

Thus the situation is of one group of fossils which represent creatures which lived before the main volcanic activity began in areas which were later buried beneath the volcano. The second group records a growing volcano with vegetation and animals living on the slopes of the cone in periods when the volcano was dormant. Later the fossil material was buried and stratified in ash falls and later again the Napak volcano was eroded down to its present remnant state.

The animals which lived in Uganda in association with the Primates during the Lower Miocene period included an elephant, or rather a Proboscidean in the form of the early mastodon *Trilophodon angustidens* which possessed fairly massive tusks and teeth which are very different from those of the modern African elephant in that they are composed of pairs of cones. The carnivores included a large creature called *Pterodon*, about the same size as a tiger with very pronounced shearing teeth, and also a carnivore resembling *Amphicyon*, an early dog-like creature. The preservation of the fossils is very good and as at other East African Miocene sites remains of small mammals are very numerous. Rodents are particularly abundant and include creatures broadly reminiscent of the modern guinea-pig and the flying squirrel in addition to other forms. Chalicotheres, Ruminants, Rhinoceroses and Insectivores are also represented. From these fossils one can build up a picture of the fauna contemporary with the Primates. The majority of the bones have already been broken before fossilization and many show signs of chewing and gnawing by carnivores and rodents. The assemblage consists of a rather broken up series of isolated bones although these represent a wide range of creatures. The Primate which occurs most frequently in the Uganda Lower Miocene is the unspecialized ape *Proconsul* which is also known from many of the Kenya Miocene sites. A skull of *Proconsul* was found by Mrs. Leakey on Rusinga Island in Kenya in 1947 and is still the oldest and best preserved fossil skull of the larger Primates. However, several teeth and jaw fragments of *Proconsul* are now known from Napak.

In 1958 Mr. Wilson, who originally discovered the Napak site, found Mastodon teeth at a site to the north of Moroto mountain, also in Karamoja. At this site again, Miocene volcanic deposits have been laid down on the crystalline rocks of the old Karamoja plain. The fossiliferous deposits represent river gravels occupying a former valley cut into that plain. The thin gravelly grits containing the fossils attain a thickness of approximately ten feet and have been sealed in beneath basaltic lava flows.

In 1961 I was fortunate to excavate at Mr. Wilson's Moroto site where I found more Mastodon teeth *in situ* in the deposit and also located another new fossiliferous deposit in a similar geological setting, two miles north of Mr. Wilson's site. The finds at this locality in August 1961 included half of the palate of the gorilla-sized ape *Proconsul major*. In December of the same year Professor Allbrook, and a party of students from the Department of Anatomy at Makerere College, revisited the site and found four further pieces of *Proconsul major* including, which was very fortunate, the other half of the original palate and two other contiguous fragments. A total of ten pieces of *Proconsul major* are now known from Napak and Moroto in Uganda to set alongside the ten original pieces from Songhor and Rusinga in Kenya.[1]

In addition to teeth of the chimpanzee-sized species *Proconsul nyanzae* the Karamoja sites have yielded smaller primates. These include *Limnopithecus* which resembles in size and

[1] Bishop, W. W., and Allbrook, D., 'New Fossil Hominoid Material from Uganda', *Nature*, vol. 197, pp. 1187–90.

Further excavations in December 1963 and January 1964 have added several more pieces to the palate and all the teeth have now been found. At Napak 26 primate fragments were found to add to the 18 previously found since 1957 and the remains of *Limnopithecus* were particularly abundant.

general form the modern gibbon, a relative of the modern wide-eyed galagos known as *Mioeuoticus*, and a few teeth of monkeys.

Following the period of these early Miocene Primates there is in Uganda a gap in the fossil evidence of almost twenty million years. Even during the early Pleistocene period commencing some one or two million years ago, the geological evidence from Uganda is still somewhat patchy.

However, one must pay tribute to the work carried out by Mr. E. J. Wayland while Director of the Geological Survey of Uganda from 1919 to 1939 and again on his return to Uganda from 1954 to 1958. On a classic safari in 1919 Wayland visited and described many areas of Uganda which have since become important in East African Pleistocene Stratigraphy. In returning from the Western Rift towards Kampala, he discovered traces of gold in the deposits of the River Kafu and also a series of what appeared to be extremely primitive 'pebble tools' to which the name 'Kafuan Culture' was given.

If this paper had been written twenty years ago the record of the early toolmakers in Uganda would undoubtedly have been said to commence with the 'Kafuan'. The nature of the industry and its raw material was later described by Van Riet Lowe. However, it is important to remember that the material for Van Riet Lowe's book was largely written in 1939 although published virtually unchanged as late as 1952.

There is no doubt that prolonged search in the pebble gravels which occur abundantly in the Kafu Valley does yield occasional fractured pebbles which are indistinguishable from the flaked pebbles undoubtedly made and used by man at all periods from that of the Chellean Culture up to the present day. However to obtain these, means that one has to select particular fractured pebbles from an environment which includes between 40 per cent. and 60 per cent. fractured and flaked pebbles in every 1,000 specimens collected at random anywhere in the Kafu Valley.[1]

In terms of abundance it appears doubtful if the so-called Kafuan tool types can be proved to be the work of man. As the stratigraphy of the Kafu gravel terraces does not support

[1] Bishop, W. W., 1959, 'Kafu Stratigraphy and Kafuan Artifacts', *South African Journ. Science*, vol. 55, pp. 117–21.

a Pre-Chellean, or Pre-handaxe culture, age for the Kafuan culture sequence this must now be disregarded in considering the prelude to the early toolmakers in Uganda. The fractured pebbles which occur in the youngest gravels of the Kafu Valley were undoubtedly flaked by man but there is no evidence which proves the existence of an earlier pebble culture of an age equivalent to, or pre-dating, the primitive choppers of the Oldowan culture.

Early in the 1920s Wayland undertook an expedition to the vicinity of the fishing village of Kaiso on Lake Albert and recovered an assemblage of early Pleistocene Mammalia, Fish, Reptilia and Molluscan fossils. More recent investigations near Kaiso have shown that the Mammalian fossils range from early to late Villafranchian in age and thus by definition these Kaiso series deposits are of earliest Pleistocene age.

The fossils seem to antedate slightly the lowest deposits of Bed I at Olduvai Gorge in Tanganyika from which Dr. and Mrs. Leakey have recently obtained fossil hominoid remains and also stone tools of the Oldowan culture.

Thus the Kaiso series of Uganda is situated near a crucial boundary in the development of man. The Uganda Museum is further investigating the Kaiso age deposits during the Baker Centenary year 1963–4 in the hope of obtaining further evidence relating to the prelude to the early Toolmakers of Uganda.

2 *The Earliest Toolmakers*

A rhetorical question which the archaeologist must answer is, 'What constitutes a tool in terms of pre-history?' There is a good deal of confusion today among prehistorians between the meaning of the word tool and the quite different word artefact. A tool as used by primitive man need not have been in any way changed from its original natural form—a pebble taken out of the river and used as a hammer-stone is a tool. True it becomes battered as a result of usage but it was not made into a pebble by man though it is still a tool. In much later contexts, such as the Iron Age, a smooth pebble picked up and used by a potter for smoothing his pottery is a tool of that potter; it has not been made into tool and it certainly was not an artefact. Artefact implies the changing of the form of a natural object for a specific purpose.

The earliest toolmakers are not synonymous with the earliest tool users and my title 'The earliest Toolmakers' implies the definite making of tools. The definition of man as Man the Toolmaker was originally worked out in London by a group of anthropologists as that stage of evolution when a certain creature began to make tools to a set and regular pattern. That definition, which was very carefully worded, was subsequently modified by Dr. Kenneth Oakley[1] but the implication was there of the making and of the changing of natural objects and changing their form and shape for a specific purpose as a regular custom and practice. With that qualified by implication or proof you could go on from there to prove that such and such a creature was Man.

But in point of fact that definition no longer holds good. In 1961 at a further symposium we had to abandon that definition. The definition is no longer valid partly because of the work of Miss Jane Goodall who is undertaking important field work on chimpanzees.[2] Miss Goodall established that in wild condi-

[1] *Man the Toolmaker*, B.M. (Natural history) handbook, 1st edition, 1949.
[2] *National Geographic Magazine*, 1963, vol. 124, pp. 272–308.

tions chimpanzees make tools to a set and regular pattern. Every October, November, and December when the rains approach they make tools of wood and of grass stem nearly all to approximately the same length, sometimes as many as six or seven. They strip off the leaves and they break off the ends. They then take these 'tools' to termite mounds which they tear down with their hands, after which they use these tools one by one to fish termites from the termites' nests. They lick the tools and put them down the termitry. The termites, attracted by the liquid of the spittal, accumulate on them, and the chimpanzees pick them off. When one stick becomes a bit damaged and bent through being pulled through the mouth too quickly, it is discarded and another one is picked up from the bundle. This has been observed for three successive years; it is not just a casual thing, they are making tools to a set pattern, tools of grass and of wood. But if chimpanzees make tools to a set and regular pattern, then clearly we must think again a great deal about what could and could not have been done by our proto-ancestors, who certainly had bigger brains than chimpanzees and were probably more advanced in their manual ability.

We have now had to amplify our definition to include the making of tools to a set and regular pattern as part of that definition and also to include a brain which is large relative to the body size. A gorilla in extreme conditions can have a brain of 700 c.c. but in a body weight of perhaps 450–500 lb. whereas the australopithecines had a fairly small brain of about 500–600 c.c. mean, but with a very small body; a brain large in relation to body size and a hand capable of at least a power grip as well as the ability of making tools to a set and regular pattern.

Tools then need not be artefacts, they can be natural objects which are used, they can also be natural objects that have been modified in shape. As far as we are concerned the earliest toolmakers were making very simple tools of stone which are preserved; a few simple tools of bone which are preserved; and we may assume that they most probably made an enormous number of tools of perishable objects which are not preserved. Now these earliest tools of the earliest known culture would probably have been called in the old days Kafuan but we have

B

abandoned the term Kafuan because most of the Kafuan 'tools' came out of the river gravels where you could not be certain that Nature had not played its part in fashioning them. It is better to call the material Early Oldowan. The principal and most typical stone tools of the culture are choppers, in a variety of shapes and forms, depending not on the desire of the man to have different shapes and forms but on the particular shape of the original pebble or nodule which he picked up to make a tool from, together with the flakes knocked from them. Many books on prehistory, still describe core-cultures and flake-cultures but there is no such division in prehistory.

Any stone-age society used cores and flakes and the more the so-called core-cultures are studied the more it is found that a high proportion of the so-called core-culture tools were either made on flakes or were accompanied by many flake tools.

It is possible with a simple tool, such as a nodule with just a minimum of flakes knocked off in two directions to give a jagged cutting edge, to skin an animal up to the size of a donkey and to dismember the whole of the dead body of that animal into various joints—in fact to do all the things you can do with an ordinary present-day steel skinning-knife. Such a tool takes only 25 to 40 seconds to make but in the course of making that tool you inevitably knock off flakes, some of which are cortex flakes and some of which are flakes that also have sharp cutting edges. With such a chopping tool of the earliest cultures although you can skin, cut up and joint an animal, there are certain things that you cannot do with it, because by its very nature the chopping tool has a thick-set edge. When you have to separate the ligaments that bind the two limb-bones of an arm or separate a tibia from a femur you find that the thick-set edge will not penetrate to cut down; and if you want to do that effectively, you pick up one of the cortex flakes, that you knocked off in making your chopper for your main work, and with that you can sever those ligaments. But you could not do that with only the chopper which explains why on all living sites of the earliest known stone cultures you find both choppers and enormous numbers of waste flakes, on a proportion of which there is clear evidence of utilization and on a further proportion of which there is actual trimming to modify them for additional purposes. You also find with these cultures a proportion of bones that have definitely been used, sometimes modified before use and employed apparently for rubbing leather thongs to soften them. Bones were used for digging as abrasion of the point clearly shows under the microscope and there must also have been wooden tools.

To what extent, if you find stone tools, bone tools and broken-up bones of animals on a sealed-in living floor of very early Pleistocene times, are you or are you not justified in saying that this living floor with these tools upon it and the fossil hominid found on the floor are in such an association that you can say that these tools were made by the creature that is represented by this skull or this jaw? This is a vital question for any student of prehistory to bear in mind because if he misinterprets the facts of the association, he will find himself in a very difficult situation from which to extricate himself. If you have only got the evidence of one single species of hominid at a given point in time and if you find the remains of that type of hominid on a sealed-in living-floor with stone tools and animal bones, given both those ifs, then you can say it seems likely or that it is probable, that this skull or that this jaw may represent the makers of the culture found on the floor in association with it. That is what we did over the study of *Zinjanthropus* in 1959. At that time we had no evidence of the existence anywhere in Africa of another type of hominid to the *Zinjanthropus/Australopithecus/Paranthropus* creature. We now know that *Paranthropus* and *Australopithecus* are later than *Zinjanthropus*. Then we felt that it was likely that *Zinjanthropus* represented the makers of the very Early Oldowan culture of core choppers, utilized flakes, and of a bone tool or two. One is entitled to say that this is a probability, provided it is made quite clear that this is only a theory to fit the facts with which one is faced. This does not mean that the discovery of stone tools with *Zinjanthropus* at Olduvai proves that the australopithecines in South Africa made stone tools. They did nothing of the sort. The discovery of stone tools with *Zinjanthropus* at Olduvai does not even prove that *Zinjanthropus* made stone tools there.

When, as we have done so at Olduvai, one subsequently finds that not only on the same floor as the *Zinjanthropus* skull but also on other floors, some slightly older and some slightly younger, there exists an entirely different type of hominid with a much bigger brain and with entirely different characters in dentition and everything else, then obviously one can no longer say that it is even probable that *Zinjanthropus* made the tools found with him. There exist three possibilities: (a) that *Zinjanthropus* made the stone tools found on these various floors in the lower and middle part of Bed I and the other hominid type represented by another group of fossils made none; (b) that the large-brained other type of creature made all the tools and *Zinjanthropus* made none; (c) that both types of hominid were toolmaking, one having imitated the other. Primates, whether they are monkeys or anything else are very inclined to copy. For the moment, on purely theoretical grounds, we think that it is distinctly possible that both made the tools, one making tools rather better than the other. A most remarkable fact emerges from a close study of the stone tools that were found on the *Zinjanthropus* floor with the Zinjanthropus skull—the best made are less well made than the average tools found at a much lower level at the place where the human remains represent the other type of creature. We think that it is more than probable that *Zinjanthropus* was copying the tools of the other type of creature who probably invented the idea, but we cannot say for certain. These are purely three possibilities, any of which may be correct.

Toolmaking, when it comes to things like the chopping-tool, requires at least a power grip. Chimpanzees making their simple tools are not using a power grip or a precision grip. Part of the toolmaking is done with the lips, part with the hands by drawing the stems between the thumbs and the fingers to strip off the leaves and then breaking them, but the breaking is done in a very crude manner, using neither a precision grip nor a power grip. To use a chopper or a waste flake knocked off a chopper, for severing the tendons between the two bones of a leg or an arm, one requires to have at least a power grip in which the tool is held in a very precise way (Plate 1). In certain circumstances chimpanzees can grip but the objects can be pulled away from them so that it cannot be said that they have a power grip. The making and the using of choppers implies a power grip.

Olduvai is a gorge in northern Tanganyika some 35 miles long which in its deeper parts is over 300 feet deep with Stone Age cultures from the lowest levels, resting upon the lava, right through to the top. In 1951 it was thought that there were twelve stages of culture, we now know that in Bed 1 alone there are at least seven. Whereas before we had only one stage in the lower 15 feet of Bed 2 we now have no less than four distinct stages. The total cultural stages represented in the whole Olduvai sequence, each stratigraphically separated from the other, is likely to be of the order of thirty-five. In this account we are only concerned with the top of Bed 1 and the bottom of Bed 2.

But what of the toolmakers? First of all, if good evidence of a sealed-in living-floor is to be obtained, there is a need to find a living-site where man was living by the edge of water, a lake or river, where he left his tools and the bones of the animals he fed upon. Later that site would need to be sealed-in quickly enough for the bones and stones to be preserved instead of being dissipated either by decay or erosion. Such a site is the *Zinjanthropus* site at Olduvai and on that living-floor there are the bones of the animals which were eaten by the creatures which lived there, together with the stone tools that he made there and the waste flakes that he knocked off in making the tools and the hammer stones and everything else, not in tens or hundreds but literally in thousands.

Zinjanthropus was certainly a creature of the type of hominid which is known in science as the Australopithecines, a subfamily of the hominids, which was first discovered and described in South Africa at Taungs and subsequently from Sterkfontein, Makapans, Kromdraai and several other places. The characteristics of the australopithecines include a very small brain (*Zinjanthropus's* brain is only 570 c.c.) a relatively long face, a very massive lower jaw resulting in very projecting zygomatic arches and enormously big molars and pre-molars and small incisors and canines, which when compared with the other teeth are very small. Some of the male australopithecines, both *Zinjanthropus* and some from South Africa, have a sagittal crest of bone on the head which does not extend right to the front of the skull. This, however, is not of any taxonomic significance; it is purely functional. If a creature has an enormously massive jaw with enormously massive temporal muscles extending over the wall of the parietals then inevitably if those muscles are big enough they will go right up to the middle line and then, whether it is a hyena or a dog or a leopard or a lion or a primate, if those muscles get sufficiently big the crest of bone gets built up along the sagittal suture to take the load of those muscles. These australopithecines were also remarkably low browed.

Zinjanthropus has a longer face than any of the South African members of the sub-family, he has a much bigger and much more human mastoid and the mastoid process is as in present-day man. He has another characteristic which distinguishes him from the South African australopithecines, which is why he has a different sub-generic rank. His teeth are enormous compared with the teeth of a modern man. The incisors of present-day man are if anything smaller than those of *Zinjanthropus* whose canines are bigger than those of any known man. The *Zinjanthropus* jaw is also characterized by greatly reduced anterior teeth. The australopithecines have a strange feature in that the parietals come down, they have not yet expanded out to come truly above the mastoid. The mastoid process is carried as it were on a shelf projecting sideways from the parietal area because the brain had not yet filled out. Seen from above the australopithecines when quite properly oriented in the Frankfort plane are very little prognathous. *Zinjanthropus* is less prognathous than any of the others and when oriented in the Frankfort plane the anterior part of the maxilla, which is between the base of the nose and the front teeth, hardly projects forward from the most projecting part of the top of the skull.

There is another characteristic which is most interesting and which in *Zinjanthropus* is even more highly emphasized. The face of the present-day man is barely half the length of that of *Zinjanthropus*, on the other hand the nasal spines are as strongly developed as they are in present-day man whereas they are not in the australopithecines of South Africa. The premaxillary height, the height from the spines to the front teeth, is exceptionally great, the greatest known in any hominid anywhere; the zygomatic width is also enormous, a very peculiar feature and altogether fundamentally unprecedented.

In 1960, on a living-floor ((FLK. NN.1) which also yielded

Sabre-toothed tiger, some twenty feet below the uppermost limit of Bed 1, a large part of a lower jaw of a juvenile was located. The interesting thing about this pre-*Zinjanthropus* jaw is that the canines are so enormous that it was first thought by Le Gros Clark to be a pongid. The canine is quite unlike that of *Australopithecus* as are its pre-molars since all the pre-molars of *Australopithecus* are much wider buco-lingually (from side to side) than they are long from back to front. In this creature the pre-molars are long from back to front and rather narrow from side to side, in this respect they rather resemble the molars of *Proconsul*. The proportion of the molars is different and also the cusp arrangement. This little jaw cannot represent an australopithecine, it is much closer to present-day man.

With the jaw are the parietals, from the same individual one rather more complete than the other. Fortunately the part that is missing in the more complete one is duplicated in the other which has the front part missing so that we can get an exact reconstruction of the parietals. The parietals are those of a child probably not more than eleven years old, or perhaps less, which has at least 5 per cent. growth to come. The parietals can fit perfectly on the brain cast of a *Pithecanthropus* No. 2 from Java, a man who had a brain capacity of about 1,000 c.c. This represents then a creature that had a bigger brain than *Zinjanthropus*, which is a big-brained australopithecine of only 570 c.c.[1] This, then, is a creature whose dentition and jaw structure is completely unaustralopithecine with parietals which indicate, even for a child, a brain capacity of up to 1,000 c.c. and in an adult certainly more than that. The hand bones indicate a child whose proximal epipheses had not yet fused. The hand, as a result of detailed study, is clearly not pongid but retains a number of pongid characters. This creature certainly had a power grip,[2] which neither a gorilla nor a chimpanzee has, but probably had still not got a true precision grip as the tools also indicate. The terminal phalanges of the thumb are indistinguishable from those of Man.

[1] Many of the former estimates of the brain capacities of the australopithecines are inaccurate as they were based on an unreliable method using Martin's index.

[2] Napier, J., *Nature*, vol. 196, pp. 409–11, 'Fossil hand bones from Olduvai Gorge'.

Found accompanying these bones was the foot of an adult female. The whole of the phalanges of this foot had been chewed away as had the distal ends of the metatarsals. The calcanium is also missing but the heel and the ankle survived as well as a greater part of the structure of the foot. As a result of study it is possible to say that this foot is well within the range structurally and morphologically of the feet of present-day men and women. It is smaller, but it is not anything like as primitive as that of the man found on the same horizon as the child. The evidence suggests most strongly that in evolution, the foot, and with the foot upright stature, came before the full development of the hand. This is what you would expect. You would not expect the hand to develop until the foot and the hip were sufficiently well developed into something approaching that of present-day man which enabled the creature to be free of having to use his arms or his hands to support his weight at any point. The foot is much more advanced than the hand in those creatures found with tools of the Oldowan culture in a slightly lower horizon geologically, but to all intents and purposes of the same age.

We now have from the *Zinjanthropus* floor teeth and bits of a skull which certainly belong to this type of creature, so that even on the *Zinjanthropus* floor the two hominid types were contemporary. Did the big-brained type kill the *Zinjanthropus* because he had invaded the camp and then left him lying on the fringes to be eaten by the vultures and small creatures? Or, did *Zinjanthropus*, whose skull is very complete on his floor, die there after being wounded by some animal in the hunt, having crawled back home to die, and his skull remained on the floor on the fringes of the camp? Do the teeth and parts of the skull of the different creature found on that floor represent part of his food, with *Zinjanthropus* feeding on the bigger-brain type when he was lucky enough to kill one? We just don't know.

The foot of the female creature represented a being who was much smaller than present-day woman and would have taken a shoe number 2 in size which only four per 1,000 of present-day women take. The collar-bone of this second type of creature is known from two specimens and is indistinguishable from that of present-day man. This is an entirely *Homo sapiens* type of collar-bone and derives from a horizon rather lower than that of *Zinjanthropus* even on the *Zinjanthropus* floor.

These then were the earliest toolmakers that we know so far, not only from East Africa, but from anywhere in the world. They go back well into the Lower Pleistocene, with a date based on the potassium–argon technique of 1,750,000 years. They were making very simple tools and using them at least with a power grip with which they could skin an animal very efficiently, using the waste flakes knocked off from the choppers to sever the ligaments between joints.

This now brings us to the status of the South African 'stone-age' claims made for certain discoveries supposed to be associated with australopithecines. A very important paper has just been published by Robinson and Mason in the *South African Archaeological Bulletin*[1] discussing the significance of stone tools from the Middle Sterkfontein levels in the Transvaal. The Lower Sterkfontein levels have yielded vast numbers of remains of a true australopithecine, formerly called *Plesianthropus*, now called *Australopithecus*, but it is not a genus separate from the Taungs and Makapans type. But no tools of either stone or bone have been found in the Lower Sterkfontein levels. The Middle Sterkfontein levels, originally discovered by Dr. Brain and worked by Dr. Mason, have now yielded something like 300 stones of foreign origin of which at least 200 are artefacts though there are natural stones, which have subsequently been altered in shape, amongst them. There is also one complete and several broken true handaxes, which I should call Chellean II. In this same breccia are nine hominid teeth which Robinson says represent an *Australopithecus*. I should say they represent a hominid or, question mark hominid. There is not enough evidence to denote genus, let alone species. The associated animal fauna is quite different from the fauna in the lower levels which yielded the quantities of true australopithecines.

There are two possibilities for the situation in the Sterkfontein Middle levels—one is the hypothesis published by Robinson that these are fragments of australopithecines associated with the type of handaxes found at Olduvai. But in this breccia there are many blocks and derived fossils from the lower breccia. The teeth, if they are australopithecine, may have been

[1] Vol. XVII (1962), pp. 87–127.

derived into the middle breccia from the breakdown of the earlier lower breccia. But there is no proof—and Robinson says this and underlines it—that the teeth represent the makers of those handaxes. In South Africa in middle breccia times you have very well-preserved remains of three different individuals of a creature which Broom originally called *Telanthropus* but which Robinson now calls *Homo erectus*, a true Man. So this means that both in South Africa as in East Africa there is evidence of two different types of contemporaneous hominid not only at the beginning of the middle Pleistocene but well down in the upper part of the Lower Pleistocene. There is, therefore, a grave series of question-marks as to who made what tools.

It is a burning question in the anthropological journals as to whether one can have two contemporary hominids side by side anywhere in the world. You can have gorillas and chimpanzees side by side and you have four or five different kinds of monkey side by side in a single forest and so to say that it is impossible, as a dogma or as an article of faith, that you cannot have two different type of hominids side by side is ridiculous. The beginning of the Pleistocene was a period when a great burst of evolution of mammals was still in force; since then there has been a great dying off of many genera and species of mammals but at the time of the lower beds of Olduvai there were no less than 19 different species of pigs, representing seven genera and there were something like fifty different types of antelope. There were also enormous numbers of other different creatures representing much smaller numbers. It was a time of experiment in nature in the mammal field. We cannot afford in our science preconceived ideas, we are only beginning to learn a whole host of things we did not know about.

These early toolmakers were living by water. Why? Why do all our early sites of earliest known man occur near places where there was then water? You can carry solid objects, once you are standing upright; you can carry meat, you can carry bone, you can carry skins and you can carry stones to make stone tools with, but our hands are insufficient to carry water in an adequate quantity. There were still no vessels in which to carry water so man lived by the edges of lake shores. Because he lived by the edge of fluctuating lakes there was a higher chance that his sites would be sealed in before the bones were destroyed by decay. An increase in precipitation and the lake level rises and the floor is sealed in by clays and silts; if with waters charged with minerals, then the bones are preserved. So man lived by water, by the water supply of the hunter and his family.

On the floors, if one is lucky enough to find them sealed in, as we have done at Olduvai, one finds that the bones which carry a big marrow hollow inside them are invariably broken and smashed to smithereens to extract the marrow. One finds on the *Zinjanthropus* floor utilized waste flakes and chopping tools together with broken-up bones split to get the marrow out. Where there was a femur articulated to a tibia or a humerus articulated to a radia and ulna, man seems to have separated those bones with extreme care at this early stage because he wanted to get the last bit of meat from them. Later he would break them up and get the marrow out. But he very seldom took the trouble to separate out the ligaments and counter ligaments of say the calcanium, astragalus and foot-bones of an antelope. There was nothing worth getting at there, neither marrow nor flesh. Again and again on these living-floors it is possible to find discarded articulated joints from those parts of the limbs where there was nothing worth getting at or no marrow to extract. Skulls were broken up to get at the brain and as far as the face was concerned to get at the tongue and the meat we still use from many animals to make brawn with. But the horn cores were left intact since again there was nothing worth getting.

On these living-floors the distribution of 'tools' is fantastic and includes stones that have been brought there, which I term maniports, or something which has been carried there and has not been altered in shape or form. A maniport is quite distinct from an artefact and was carried there for a purpose. Some of them were used as tools and hammers. Man was, therefore, from the evidence of the floors, killing and eating large animals. Did he kill those large animals himself or was he a scavenger? Probably both. He certainly did some scavenging but the likelihood is that he also did some killing with his bare hands. Miss Goodall's work shows that chimpanzees regularly kill small animals with their hands. They kill colobus monkeys, they kill small pigs and small bushbuck. But if chimpanzees are hunters

with their hands, how much more so would *Zinjanthropus* and
the other hominids have been. I have also caught and killed
small antelopes with my hands and I have also caught hares
with my bare hands and if I can, and I am not hungry, how
much more so could *Zinjanthropus* when he was hungry and
when his children were crying out for food. There is certainly
no sign of any lethal weapon amongst these artefacts of the
earliest toolmakers.

But they also killed small creatures, rats, mice, lizards, frogs,
chameleons, fishes, small birds and snakes. Small patches of
concentrated bones of minute animals have been found on the
Olduvai FLN level, the level of the jaw and of the foot of the
other type of hominid. These patches are almost solid with the
bones of small creatures. I am almost certain now as the result
of experiment that they represent patches of human dung
passed through the intestines. The creatures have been caught,
chewed and digested, but not digested in the way that a carnivore does. If you take the dung of a cat or dog or of a hyena,
boil it and sort it out there will be practically no bones left at
all, because the bone is completely destroyed by the stomach
acids. But if a man does the same thing experimentally and eats
whitebait or small birds and chews up the whole bird, then
broken-up bone is passed through the intestines in quantity.
These patches therefore represent patches of human faeces on
the floors, concentrated meals of small birds, rats and mice
deposited on the outskirts of the living-site as dung. There is a
lot more research to be done on this problem and it would
seem that another part of the early toolmaker's diet was small
creatures.

It is very noticeable that on these sites the bones that do not
carry marrow, such as the cannon-bone of an ape, which if you
break them are pretty well solid, have not been broken up.
There can thus be no doubt about man's selectivity of bones.
A question that is often asked is whether early man lived in
shelters of any sort. For a long time it has been assumed that
he lived out in the open and many prehistorians have thought
that he lived in this respect like any other animal but the recent
research of primatologists into the behavioural patterns of
various creatures show that gorillas, chimpanzees and other
primates have definite shelters or sleeping-platforms. Work in

1962 on the DK I site has revealed a mass of stones in an arcuate form. The deposits at this site are all fine grained, so the boulders, many of which are quite large, measuring up to twelve inches across, must have been brought into the site by man. It is possible that they formed a simple windbreak and it is not inconceivable that once the stones had been piled up, poles picked up from near the site were inserted to add effectiveness.

In Bed 2 (site LLK II) a third hominid site was found associated with a Chellean III industry. The main find was the upper part of a skull, minus the face and lower portions. The creature had a domed skull, the frontal area being greater than that of the Pithecanthropines. The remains found at Broken Hill in mining operations and known as *Homo Rhodesiensis* are the nearest parallel in Africa as regards the brow ridges. Other features are the short occipital region and the relative broadness immediately behind the tremendous brow ridge; whilst the forehead itself is wide. From the front there is a similarity to the finds from Steinheim in Europe. At this site men of the Chellean culture had 'bolas' stones weighing up to twenty-eight pounds.

This is the first well-authenticated find of the type of man living in Africa when the first handaxes were being made. By this time man had been firmly established as a toolmaker for the best part of a million years and was already an accomplished hunter. Though Olduvai Gorge has been excavated since 1931, the fossil hominid finds, except for an isolated tooth in 1955, have only been made since 1959 and much more remains to be discovered about the earliest toolmakers from the intensive study of his sites that we are now engaged in undertaking.

EDITOR'S POSTSCRIPT

Recent finds published in *Nature* (for 4 April 1964) have brought the number of hominid finds from Olduvai to sixteen whilst a mandible of an australopithecine, the first from East Africa, was found at a new site on the west side of Lake Natron in January 1964. The pre-*Zinjanthropus* skull fragments have a mean cranial capacity of around 680 c.c., close to the range of true man (*Homo erectus* lowest cranial capacity, 775 c.c.).

On the basis of the new finds Dr. Leakey, Dr. Napier and Professor P. V. Tobias have redefined the genus *Homo* and described the species *Homo habilis* of which there are possibly six representatives at Olduvai. The cranial capacity of the new species, which is the contemporary of *Zinjanthropus* referred to as Pre-Zinj in the foregoing chapter, is smaller than *Homo erectus* to which the pithecanthropines belong, the canines are larger relative to the pre-molars, and the hand-bones, though robuster than those of *Homo sapiens*, would still allow a rudimentary precision grip. It is suggested that *Telanthropus carpensis*, the Kanam mandible and possibly the remains from near Lake Chad, previously described as *Australopithecus*, are members also of the species *Homo habilis*. Leakey suggests that the windbreak at DK I and the stone tools of the Oldowan culture are the work of *Homo habilis*. The LLK II site hominid has now been assigned to *Homo erectus pithecanthropus*.

The Early Stone Age—an Interpretative Approach

The Stone Age in Africa began with the earliest attempts at making stone tools some one and a half million years ago and continued until almost the nineteenth century in certain parts of the continent. The terminology of the Stone Age is based on technological changes as reflected in cultures named from type sites where a particular culture was first differentiated. To some extent the subdivisions are based on stratigraphy. The terminology arrived at for Africa differs from that of Europe in that the terms, palaeolithic and mesolithic are not used and in their place are the Early, Middle and Late Stone Ages with a First Intermediate period between the Early and Middle Stone Age and a Second Intermediate period between the Middle and Late Stone Ages. (Table 1).

The Early Stone Age, which lasted until about 50,000 years ago, was characterized by the use of standardized tools particularly as evidenced in the development of the handaxe, and by the absence of fire, and by the association in time with a largely extinct fauna of the Lower and Middle Pleistocene period. In the Later Stone Ages the animal species of the Upper Pleistocene were virtually as at the present time, specialized tools were in use and we are dealing with a human species of the present *Homo sapiens* type.

Several general observations can be made about the Stone Age in Africa. With the emergence of the earliest toolmakers of the australopithecine stock, human evolution proceeded at a rapid pace. It can to some extent be said that Man domesticated himself. Selection was no longer a natural process but depended more on Man's ability to transmit ideas, his adaptability to different environments, and on his success as a hunter, using and developing the techniques of making his tools and co-operating with others of his group. Group activity and the transmission of ideas demanded language, and language was probably a development of Stone Age man. These hunters progressed from the creatures with a brain of 600 c.c. and the massive 'nutcracker' jaw of the man of Olduvai to the Rhodesian Man of the Middle Stone Age with a brain of 1,300 c.c.

Much of this rapid evolution took place in Africa and Africa was in some respects the centre of the Stone Age world. Whereas in Europe the first tools are post Oldowan, in Africa the whole process of the development of the handaxe industries took place. The pace of change was slow, perhaps the first tools were made one and a half million years ago, the first handaxes (Chellean) between 300,000 and 500,000 years ago, whilst the full development of the handaxe (Acheulean) industries cannot be dated much before 100–200,000 years ago. Africa was probably then the most populous continent, though it has been estimated[1] that the Early Stone Age population of Africa was not more than 125,000 and that even by the end of the Late Stone Age a hunting economy could not have supported more than 3 or 4 million people at the most.

When we link these population figures with the length of time involved in the Early Stone Age we have to reckon with a population of over 50,000,000,000 hunters during the period, all of whom left indestructible tools behind them. Stone tools are heavy, they easily lose their edge and must have been made for the job in hand rather than carried from site to site. On several Early Stone Age living-floors, where the dismembered remains of large animals have been found, large numbers of good tools such as cleavers and handaxes have been discovered indicating that they were used to butcher the creatures, whose bones have survived, and then left behind. This was something that must have happened almost daily and if we multiply our number of hunters by only 5,000 to represent the number of handaxes, cleavers or choppers made by a single hunter in an active mature life of perhaps fifteen years we have a staggering figure of 250,000,000,000,000,000 for the probable number of stone tools left scattered over the surface of Africa from the Early Stone Age and this excludes the waste flakes which would number anything between twenty and fifty for every good tool. Much of the waste of course was utilized for making scrapers and knives, for preparing skin and animal products, and for

[1] Deevey, Edward S., Jnr., *Scientific American*, September 1960.

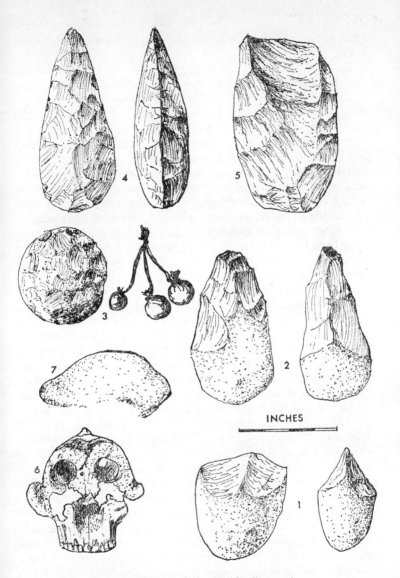

Figure I Tools of the Early Stone Age

1 Oldowan chopping tool on a pebble   **2** Chellean handaxe   **3** 'Bolus' stone with possible reconstruction   **4** Acheulean handaxe   **5** Acheulean cleaver   **6** *Zinjanthropus*   **7** Skull of Chellean man from Olduvai   (Nos. 6 and 7 not to scale and based on photographs) sharpening wooden spears for throwing or for placing in pit traps.

By and large the distribution of Man in the Early Stone Age as evidenced by his stone tools was in the Savannah zone. Few finds have been made in the forested areas and few, until the developed Acheulean industries at the end of the period, in the desert regions. This habited zone was until only recently still teeming with game, and is a zone, particularly on the fringes of the forest, where man's primate ancestors still live in abundance. The size of the living-floors indicates small communities who were probably living more by food-gathering than by actual hunting. As hunting prowess improved the proportion of the diet provided by hunting would also have increased.

Unfortunately the distribution pattern is uneven. More sites have been found in the rift valley regions than elsewhere. Lake basins existed in the unstable rift valley zones and those which were filled up with deposits in Early and Middle Pleistocene times have been cut through by Late Pleistocene and modern streams as at Olduvai and Isimila in Tanzania or Olorgesailie and Kariandusi in Kenya. Tools and fossils eroded from the deposits and visible on the surface have helped the archaeologists to discover the old land surfaces and living-floors of early Man. The lakes, except for Olduvai, were in existence for only relatively short periods and due to the relatively gentle nature of the shallow lake waters the living sites have been scarcely disturbed and the preservation of bone is good. River valleys in which the gravels incorporate material washed from the banks are another source of sites but in the areas intervening, sites are few.

From the simple Oldowan tools it was a straightforward step to the first true handaxes in which two sharp edges converged to form a point. In time, with more skill, the tools became flatter and the edges straighter. A big advance was made when it was realized that a piece of bone or wood, which is less brittle than stone, would flake in a more efficient manner than a pebble and due to their 'elasticity' the force would be spread over a wider area to remove a flatter and broader flake. It is largely this technological change which has been used to distinguish the Chellean from the Acheulean cultures though both are part of the essential continuity of the handaxe cultural-tradition.

With the Acheulean handaxes are often found associated similarly bifacially flaked tools with a straight edge at right angles, or at a slant, to the long axis. These are called cleavers whilst single side-edged tools must have served as knives. Carefully rounded stone balls were perhaps used singly as throwing stones or bound together in twos and threes to make a bolas such as are still used in South America. Even after the 'pebble tool' cultures, choppers and pounders were used. The handaxe was probably a general-purpose tool for cutting up meat and some woodworking whilst the cleaver could have been used for skinning or even used as a kind of primitive handadze. The raw materials most generally sought were fine-grained rocks like quartzites, the black volcanic glass obsidian, and quartz. Crystalline granites were unsuitable as the edge would have been too crumbly.

Many sites show different assemblages of tools. Sometimes the difference may indicate that a different activity was undertaken where large or small tools may have been less essential. At the present day when the rains come many hunters engage in swamp fishing and fowling rather than in hunting game. Many of the different cultures like the Hope Fountain probably only indicate such a variation. Some of the differences were due to the use of different kinds of raw materials. Where only pebbles were available the tools were small whilst at some sites, like Isimila, where fine-grained volcanic rocks were present, some handaxes achieved the unwieldy length of more than a dozen inches and could only have been used in two-handed fashion as digging-tools. A great abundance of broken rock, as in the scree of the Uganda site of Nsongezi, led to an abundance of crudely made tools whilst scarcity necessitated a greater care.

Hunting was probably conducted by means of drives, the animals being stampeded into lake muds or into a prepared hole where they could be killed at close range with wooden spears or stones. Scavenging probably continued well into the Early Stone Age and most of the elephant, hippopotamus and other large creatures were possibly animals butchered after dying a natural death. On the Kagera river, at Olduvai gorge and at Olorgesailie definite evidence exists to indicate that fish, mostly of the swamp variety, were caught.

The Acheulean and earlier living-sites are correlated both on the typology of the tools themselves and on the associated faunal remains. Formerly, when the existence of most of the Rift Valley lakes was thought to be due to pluvial activity, correlations were also made on the basis of climatic change. Though a greater rainfall is evident from sites like Olorgesailie where present precipitation would be insufficient to support a lake, even if a basin existed, there is insufficient data to erect a firm correlation on the basis of pluvials. Faunal correlations and correlations by *isotopic* dating are the most satisfactory ways of comparing sites. At certain localities, such as Olduvai, handaxe Man was the contemporary of various large animals now extinct like *Pelorovis*, a huge sheep, various large pigs, *Sivatherium*, a giraffid with horns, *Simopithecus*, a huge baboon and several other creatures. Possibly ideal conditions for these types of animals then existed, perhaps a damper climate with more luxuriant vegetation. Or it may have been that this was just a temporary ecological balance in favour of these large creatures. It is possible that the many volcanoes in the area contributed fresh minerals to the soil which favoured vegetation or animal growth. The reason for the extinction of these animals is again not clear—possibly drier conditions adversely affected the ecological balance or it may have been Man who played his part in their extinction. One suggestion is that natural gases in the rift valley areas where they flourished had a harmful effect.

Dating by 'absolute' methods is less useful for the Earlier Stone Age than for later periods. At present radiocarbon dating has been employed for arriving at a terminal date for the Acheulean of around 50,000 B.C. potassium argon dating methods evolved since 1957, though applied extensively to the Olduvai succession, have only a limited validity due to the large variable error for more recent samples and the need for fresh volcanic material in the deposit containing the artefacts. Unfortunately this means that only certain sites can provide dating material. Nevertheless the results so far provide a valuable indication of age which has supplemented the relative sequence built up by more straightforward stratigraphical means.

At present East Africa is inadequately prospected for remains of the past and few Early Stone Age sites have been found beyond the general rift valley areas, the Kagera river and isolated sites by Lake Victoria. Caves were not used. Fire seems to have come into use in Africa around 50,000 B.C. and allowed Man to become more adaptable. It was also about this time that new methods of making stone tools were developed in which an emphasis was placed on smaller tools. Instead of choppers, handaxes, cleavers and bolases the tools were lighter —small knives, lance heads and what must have been a wide variety of woodworking tools. The increased adaptability allowed Man to live in climates and at altitudes which he had not previously been able to tolerate. During the Early Stone Age handaxe makers had spread into both Europe and Asia and with this spread and the greater stimulus there of more exacting physical conditions, the centre of gravity of material advancement moved north of the Sahara. In general, cultural impulses and ideas were later to spread into Africa. There is also some evidence to suppose that the First Intermediate period in parts of Africa may have been a drier period and the spread into higher areas, such as the Mount Kenya foothills, or into the more heavily vegetated areas of Nyanza and the lake fringes, may have been forced by the drying up of many of the inland lakes.

4 Olorgesailie. An investigation into the Natural History of Early Men

A century of biological and geological research has established organic evolution as a fact. It is certain that mankind is derived from more animal-like ancestors by the modification of successive generations. This means in turn that the complex technology and social organizations that have become such a prominent feature of human life must have had relatively simple early stages. Archaeological study of the Old Stone Age is concerned with gaining an understanding of the formative period of human achievement. Good evidence is rare and often very difficult to interpret. Herein lies the importance of sites such as Olorgesailie.

Investigations have been proceeding there since the effective discovery of the site by Dr. and Mrs. L. S. B. Leakey in 1942, and yet because of the scale of the undertaking, interpretation of the site remains incomplete. At the present time, an intensive programme of work is under way in order to bring our knowledge to such a state that an outline of the geology, biology and anthropology can be published, and serve as a starting point for more detailed work in future. What is here attempted is not so much a report on the results of researches, as an exposition of the way in which scientists set about gleaning knowledge of the behaviour of our early ancestors.

Olorgesailie is situated in the eastern Rift Valley, some forty miles south-west of Nairobi on the road to Lake Magadi. Due to the enthusiasm and energy of Dr. Leakey and a succession of Wardens, including Mr. d'Giustina, Dr. Posnansky and Mr. Wright a small park has been built up where covered excavations and exhibits illustrate the lives of men of more than a hundred thousand years ago, and point to the importance of Africa as an early home of mankind. This field Museum is under the guardianship of the National Parks of Kenya, but is now being administered by the Museums Trustees of Kenya.

The principal relics of ancient man in the Olorgesailie area are stone tools, made in the Acheulean tradition. The archaeological story began there when earth movements connected with the formation of the Rift Valley created a basin of low-lying ground without any drainage exits. In this lake basin silts accumulated to a depth of nearly 200 feet. Men and animals were attracted by the lake and swamps, so that camping litter and carcasses often came to be covered by fresh layers of silt, and so incorporated in a natural filing system. Many such ordered storehouses of prehistory exist in East Africa, but few are as accessible for research. In this case, however, minor earth movements in recent times broke open the lake basin and exposed lines of section through the deposits. (Plate 4.)

Research begins with the discovery of a favourable geological situation—in the case of Olorgesailie this was partially accomplished by Gregory in 1919,[1] who first reported the occurrence of handaxes but did not become effective until the rediscovery by Dr. and Mrs. Leakey in 1942. The first stage of the work consists of walking over the surface exposures in search of indications of buried concentrations of fossils and artefacts. The relationship of scattered sites to one another can only be established as a result of painstaking geological study, here achieved by Dr. R. M. Shackleton.

From reconnaissance there springs an idea of the kind of archaeological evidence that is available. The evidence can only be satisfactorily obtained by systematic excavation, but the success of the excavation in elucidating life in early times, depends on the formulation of pertinent questions about the past that are capable of being answered. Thus at Olorgesailie there have been excavated or surveyed for excavation a great range of sites. Some were used time and again over a period of many years, so that finds from them represent a cross-section of tool-making practices, and feeding habits, and give information as to what constituted favourite camping conditions. One such site recently explored is on the end of a rocky promontory projecting out into the lake basin. At another site a phenomenal concentration of many thousands of large tools, in an area less than an acre, is suggestive of repetitive gatherings or 'jam-

[1] Gregory, J. W., *The Rift Valleys and Geology of East Africa* (London 1921), p. 221.

borees', at this one recognized spot. Current excavations are directed to investigating the size of the individual occupations on this site, and studying the topography which attracted such densities of people. One concentration has been found to have a diameter of about twenty yards, being contained in a hollow or runnel, and to be characterized by the remains of a single animal species—in this case an extinct baboon. The whole area in question seems to have been a sandy patch traversed by many small streams and rivulets. Unfortunately these streams have often disturbed the details of the archaeological evidence.

Other classes of sites offer glimpses into mere moments of prehistoric time. At one, the carcass of a hippopotamus lies dissected and dismembered; around it are a few stone tools, presumably those blunted beyond resharpening during a few days of carefree butchering and meat-eating.

The technology of a Stone Age people is of great importance in assessing their status and relationships to other such groups. Many aspects of their stone industry can only be studied at the source of the raw material. 'Factory' sites have been located in the Olorgesailie basin and in due course will have to be excavated.

We hope to come to an accurate reconstruction of the environment in which Acheulean men lived at Olorgesailie, from the combination of lists of terrestrial and aquatic faunas and floras, which are preserved in the lake-silts. This involves the collecting of specimens of diatomites, snail shells, animal bones, and if possible, pollen-bearing clays and muds; and their subsequent study by specialist biologists.

The investigations at Olorgesailie are unlikely to revolutionize our ideas about the development of culture, but they will contribute factual evidence in a field of thought that has largely been the preserve of speculation. To put it light-heartedly, we will not discover what our early forefathers thought about; we may not even find the mortal remains of Acheulean Man, but we are compiling *bona fide* statistics relating to his breakfast.

5 The Middle and Later Stone Age in Africa

In the study of the dawn of culture, there are two distinct aspects to be taken into account. Firstly, the human palaeontologist must assess the cultural potential of a given fossil human or sub-human type; that is, the probable competence of the creature represented by the fossil being to think, speak and to manipulate objects. Secondly, in relation to this, the archaeologist and excavator must come to an understanding of the particular mode of adaptation of that human type to gaining a living from nature through tools and habits. Evolution during the last million years has brought mankind to the state where no limit to his cultural potential can be determined either by biology or sociology. It is equally impossible to assess with any precision, the limitations of near-*sapiens* Middle Stone Age peoples. It can be assumed that during this last phase of biological evolution, natural selection assured that as fast as men's achievement approached the limit of their ability, the general level of their competence was raised by genetic changes in the population. Consequently, the closer a period is to the present, the more closely the archaeological study of it is restricted to the second of the two aspects studied in the earliest human fossils. The anthropological sciences of today are drawn upon ethnological theory in particular, and archaeology seeks to classify cultures and to understand them in terms of their ecological, geographical and historical determinants.

In Africa, the later stage in the archaeological record has been divided into a Middle Stone Age and a Later Stone Age. The details of technology and cultural content fall outside the scope of an essay such as this, but some aspects of the overall pattern that has emerged from investigation deserve treatment: most important, there was an ever-increasing tendency to regional and ecological diversity throughout the Old World, which contrasts strongly with the broad uniformity observed in the several stages of the earliest Stone Age. Properly authenticated industries of the Oldowan and Chellean phases of the Early Stone Age are extremely few, and we must suppose that populations were small and widely scattered. However, Acheulean tools are relatively common, and herein would seem to lie the key to understanding the next phase, the Middle Stone Age. Population pressure may have become such, that the more densely vegetated regions had to be colonized, and a distinctive lineage of suitably adapted cultures developed. Another effect of a new, relatively high population density may have been the strengthening of territoriality and tribalism amongst hunter-gatherer bands, which in turn may have facilitated the formation of partially isolated and distinctive variants of culture. The abundance of Middle Stone Age artefacts in Africa lends support to the idea that a population increase was involved in the transition.

Whether or not demographic factors actually affected the course of cultural evolution in the way suggested, the phenomenon of cultural diversification during the Middle and Later Stone Ages in Africa is well established. The homogeneous Acheulean handaxe tradition separated into two main lines of development, one of which was centred in the west, and the distribution of which is largely in forested and woodland regions. This is best termed 'Sangoan' from the type site area of Sango Bay on the west coast of Lake Victoria. The other tradition, which was distributed in the arc of savannah that surrounds the forest-woodland of the west and includes South Africa and the Horn, begins with industries called either 'Fauresmith' or 'Acheuleo–Levalloisian'. Good chronological evidence for the date of these transitions is scarce, but what there is suggests a period of between forty and fifty thousand years ago (see Table 1). These two streams of cultural development, though showing considerable overlap and interchange, remained distinct until the end of the Stone Age. Within each there developed very considerable regional diversity, and the rate of change became more and more rapid, so that a table representing the cultural history of Africa during the last thirty thousand years of the Stone Age is many times more complex than that representing the first million years. Despite this increasing ecological and regional variation, there is a broad

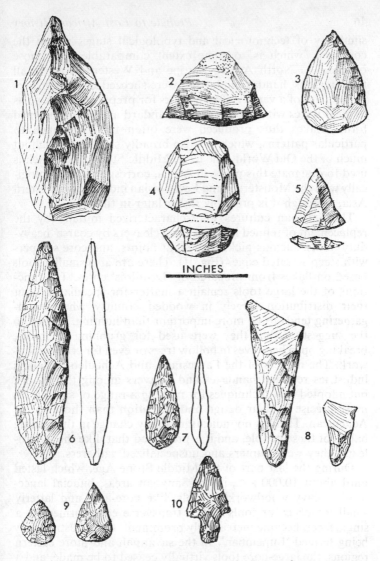

Figure II Tools of the Middle Stone Age

1 & 2 Sangoan pick and core scraper **3** Fauresmith hand-axe **4** Prepared core with levallois type flake removed **5** Flake from a longitudinal prepared core **6** Lupemban I lance **7** Lupemban II lance **8** Tranchets; early tranchets (Lupemban II) are inclined to be large, the later ones are smaller **9** Stillbay points **10** Tshitolian tanged arrowhead (Later Stone Age but following in the Lupemban tradition) similarity of technological and typological stages within the continent, which is to some extent comparable with those observed in North Africa, Europe and Western Asia. In all these regions, handaxe industries were succeeded by industries making use of a variety of techniques for preparing cores, so as to yield flakes with a more or less standard and predetermined form. Flakes thus produced were often further shaped to particular patterns, which are also broadly similar throughout much of the Old World. The term, Middle Stone Age, which is used to designate this phase in Africa, corresponds technologically with the Mousterian and Levalloisian industries of western Asia, although it is probably rather later in time.

The Sangoan cultures were characterized initially by the replacement of refined handaxes and cleavers by coarse 'heavy-duty' tools, such as picks with stout points, and core scrapers with steep serrated edges (Fig. II). There are also smaller tools based on flakes from prepared or 'Levallois' cores. The functions of the large tools remain a matter for speculation, but their distribution largely in wooded country where food-gathering tends to be more important than hunting, has led to the suggestion that they were used for grubbing up roots, breaking open bee-hives in hollow trees or even for crude wood-work. The makers of the Fauresmith and Acheuleo–Levallois industries retained handaxes and cleavers among their tools, but adopted new techniques for making a range of small tools more precise in their design and execution than those of the Acheulean. There is no indication of any change in the feeding habits of these people, and it is presumed that, like the Acheuleans, they were hunters and unspecialized gatherers.

During the last part of the Middle Stone Age, which lasted until about 10,000 B.C., in the Sangoan areas, bifacial lance-heads, heavy woodworking tools, like core-axes and latterly small *tranchets*, or tools with a transverse edge formed by a single facet, became increasingly prominent, the industries now being termed 'Lupemban'. In the savannah and more eastern regions, the large-core tools virtually ceased to be made, and a variety of bifacial and unifacial points became typical of the various 'Stillbay' industries and other cultures.

Turning to the palaeontological record it can be seen that the creators of the Acheulean culture, as far as they are known, belong to the breeding stock which gave rise to the modern races of man. Fossil men such as Swanscombe Man, Ternifine Man and the Kanjera skulls, differ amongst themselves and from the species *Homo sapiens*; but it is often thought nowadays that they are all early types within the genus *Homo*, despite the variety of Linnaean names that have been given to them in the past. The fossil men of the Upper Pleistocene and of the Middle Stone Age in Africa have formerly also been classified into numerous species of *Homo*, yet there is no real reason to suppose that there were any breeding barriers corresponding to specific divisions in zoological nomenclature. The existence of special and more or less extreme racial types such as those represented by the Rhodesian skull from Broken Hill, the Florisbad skull and the Boskop skull, is probably linked with the growth of cultural and tribal divisions in the population.

In Western Asia and Europe, the Mousterian 'prepared core' industries had been replaced, about thirty to forty thousand years ago, by industries involving new techniques and a vast array of new and specialized tools. The Upper Palaeolithic, or blade and burin industries, are associated with racial types which fall well within the range of variation shown by mankind today. This blade and burin phase has only been reported from one small area of sub-Saharan Africa—the Eastern Rift Valley of Kenya and Northern Tanzania, where it is termed the Kenya Capsian. It is best known as a result of the excavations of Dr. and Mrs. L. S. B. Leakey at Gambles Cave[1] and the Naivasha Railway rock shelter. In both cases the industries are associated with high lake levels which are attributed to maxima of the Later Pleistocene Gamblian Pluvial. The industries are refined and elaborate and largely composed of obsidian, the black volcanic glass readily found in the central area of the Kenya Rift Valley, including a variety of burins or graving tools, backed blades, crescents, blade scrapers and fragments of hardened clay which, it is suggested, may have been plastered on to basketry and subsequently burnt. Recently a fragment of a bone harpoon was discovered at Gamble's Cave. The Pleistocene age of the Kenya Capsian has been questioned on account of the crescents, the 'pottery', and the harpoon. However, geological and geophysical methods for determining the ages

[1] Leakey, L. S. B., *Stone Age Cultures of Kenya Colony* (London 1931).

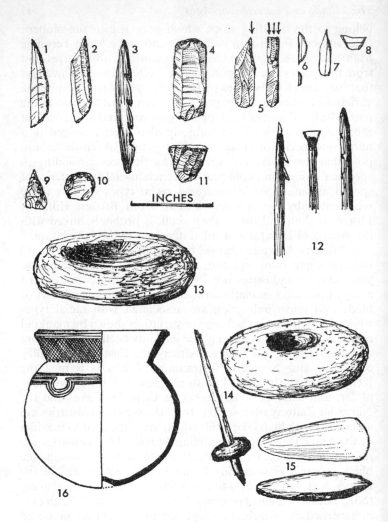

Figure III Tools of the later Stone Age

1 & 2 Backed blades of the Kenya Capsian **3** Bone harpoon from Ishango (a broken one was found at Gambles Cave Kenya and others near Lake Rudolph) **4** Capsian end-scraper **5** Capsian burin showing detachment of flakes to give chisel edge; later burins were of simpler form **6–8** Wilton microliths (6–7 crescents, 8 a trapeze) **7** Magosian point **8** Thumbnail scraper (Magosian type—smaller forms in the Wilton) **9** Bladlet core **10** Reconstructions (not to scale) showing hafting of microliths **11** Seed grinder from Magosi **12** Bored stone and reconstruction showing digging stick (not to scale) **13** Polished stone axe **14** Dimple based pot (early Iron Age) of a deposit are to be preferred to those involving only cultural criteria. It is to be hoped that this question will be settled by a series of radiocarbon determinations, and an extensive review of the geological evidence.

The Kenya Capsian industry is peculiar to a very small area, and over most of the continent, the change from Middle Stone Age to Later Stone Age was a gradual one without any break in cultural or genetic continuity. Perhaps the Kenya Capsian was the source from which many of the new techniques and ideas spread. In the eastern and savannah regions, the intermediate phase, which derives from the Stillbay, is termed 'Magosian'. Its forest-woodland counterpart is the developed 'Lupembo–Tshitolian'. This transition to the Later Stone Age took place between about 10,000 B.C. Both the industries are partially microlithic.

In Europe, Asia and North Africa, by the end of the Pleistocene about ten to twelve thousand years ago, the blade and burin industries had developed by the reduction in size of almost all tool types to minute proportions. This trend is remarkably ubiquitous during the later phases of the Pleistocene and before agriculture. No very satisfactory explanation of its cause can be offered, but it is connected with the increasing use of composite tools, made by setting small bits of stone and points in mastic on a haft, and with the manufacture of light arrows with small stone barbs. This latter use of the 'microliths', as small, precisely shaped tools are called, was dependent on the invention of the bow which, despite its importance, cannot be pin-pointed with any certainty in the archaeological record.

Thus in Africa, the Later Stone Age shows microlithic tendencies from its earliest stages and, as it is entirely post-Pleistocene, it corresponds to what is known as the Mesolithic in Europe and Asia. The best known Later Stone Age cultures of the Western forest and woodlands are the 'Tshitolian' and the 'Nachikufan'. In East Central and Southern Africa, are a series of related cultures known as the 'Wilton'. The full diversity has yet to be observed and described. From the closing millenia of the pre-Christian era, Later Stone Age hunters were influenced by contact with agricultural peoples and neolithic ideas. Pottery and ground stone tools were locally added to their equipment. In many cases, the hunting groups survived as separate entities alongside the early farmers, and utilized different aspects of the natural resources of the continent. New ecological niches were occupied by certain societies, such as the 'Strand-looping' peoples of the sea and lake shores. Populations reached a yet higher level, so that the continent is extensively littered with chips, flakes and tools typical of this period.

This is the phase of African Prehistory when traditions of painting and engraving on rocks arose and flourished in various regions and when caves and rock shelters were extensively used for habitation in contrast to the 'open' sites of the Early Stone Age.

The peoples of the Middle and Later Stone Ages were all hunters and food-gatherers. The judicious interpretation of archaeological data in the light of ethnographic knowledge of recent hunter-gatherers, can throw considerable light on the way in which Late Stone Age people lived. However, the full development of this phase of man's predatory exploitation of nature was cut short by the advent of agricultural methods, and the whole new range of social and economic structures which were thus made possible.

6 Rock Paintings in East Africa, their date and their place in African Archaeology

The story of early man in Africa rests very much on the information deduced by the archaeologists and the palaeontologists from the stray finds of his stone tools, the excavation of his living sites and the comparisons made with modern survivals of people living by hunting and food-gathering. The picture that has emerged is that of Man the Toolmaker, the Hunter but most of all Man the Wanderer in quest for his food. But what of his beliefs, his superstitions and his spiritual life? The chief source of information has and always will be the paintings and engravings on rock which are found all over Africa. At the outset it must be admitted that much of the art is mediocre in execution, conventional and unimaginative in form and for this reason the social significance of its existence and its interpretations are of greater value. The productions of the Stone Age and later artists express as stones, bones and potsherds never can the non-functional aspects of prehistoric man's existence.

The paintings of East Africa are all quite recent and essentially of the Later Stone Age though some are the work of pastoralists and agriculturalists. In the Sahara and in South Africa rock engravings are of equal importance but in East Africa few well-authenticated rock engravings have been found.

The problem of survival is important. The selection available is of a random nature. Most of the paintings are on rocks sheltered from the extremes of sun, wind and rain and though they would undoubtedly provide more comfortable working conditions for the artists there must have been innumerable areas where paintings were executed and where their exposure to the elements has destroyed them. Whereas in Europe deep caves were used where paintings survived in the ideal 'cold storage' conditions, in Africa deep caves were rarely used for habitation or even sanctuaries.

C

Suitable canvases in the main have consisted of granitic rocks, though other hard smooth surfaces have been used such as the tuffaceous agglomerate of the Elgon paintings in Kenya and the sandstone of the Bwanjai paintings in Tanganyika. Suitable canvases occur very rarely in the areas of high rainfall where exposed rock surfaces are more infrequent and the thick mantle of vegetation results in perennial streams with a small erosive capacity to undercut cliffs to form overhangs. Other canvases besides rocks such as bone, barkcloth, wood and skin were almost certainly used but none now survive.

The prerequisites for Art of any kind are ability, time, stimulation and suitable media for its execution. By the Later Stone Age Man had become a skilled toolmaker with specialized tools capable of working wood and bone. He was able to carve in the round. This increased technical skill improved his prowess as a hunter. In areas where game was abundant, life became less of the constant struggle that it had been in the Middle Stone Age. There was more leisure and a greater opportunity for conceptual thought and the complexities of social organization. The stimulation was provided by the chase, by the very form of the rounded rocks which suggested game and by the anticipation and remembrance of successful hunting days. The hunter is essentially an observer of life. His eyesight must be keen, his hearing sharp and his movements stealthy. He must possess an ability to blend with the terrain and to move ever watchful with his prey. The pricking of the ears of an animal, its every movement, its spoor, all have a significance and all must be remembered if the hunter is to learn by experience. Later Stone Age Man's hunting equipment was as rudimentary as that of the present-day Bushman. He had to lie in wait, moving as the animal moved and for ever closing in to fire his darts. Often, from a raised viewpoint like the rock shelters of the western wall of the Tanzania Rift Valley, straining his eyes over the plains and plateaux below he must have longed to create the creatures he sought. In camp amongst his family group the desire to identify himself with the animal he had successfully shot or even with the elusive prey which had deluded him must have been great and often there must have been a desire to portray the features of the animal or enact in a drawing the successful hunt.

It is impossible to suggest a simple straightforward reason why Man began to paint. The spontaneous reaction to beauty and the practical magical aim would have been complementary. The art was probably part of a very vivid folklore and profound cosmology. The artist probably found it difficult to differentiate between abstract and material things. Some of the scenes of the Tanganyika paintings can be thought of perhaps as documentary, whilst the island shelter of Lolui in Lake Victoria must have been something of a sanctuary.

How old exactly are the paintings that survive? Various methods have been employed for dating the paintings. In Zambia where geometric designs, not dissimilar to those of Uganda, occur, a spall of rock bearing these designs was found in a Nachikufan III deposit at a rock shelter near Kasama and the deposit roughly dated to around the sixteenth century A.D. At Kisese in Tanzania a spall of rock which fits into the decorated part of the overhanging rock was found in the archaeological layer suggesting a Later Stone Age date. At Nyero in Uganda a piece of bone decorated with incised concentric circles identical to designs painted in red on the rock face was found in the deposit at the foot of the rock face associated with a Late Wilton stone industry which also included Indian Ocean cowrie shells and pottery suggesting a date in the last four centuries A.D. In other parts of Africa the subject matter is a good indication of age, tropical fauna being found in desert locations or camels in North Africa.

Though elands appear on various of the Tanzania paintings where elands are not now found, we know nothing about the date when certain animals disappeared due to over-hunting. The cows and pastoral scenes of the Mount Elgon paintings do, however, suggest from comparisons with those of the Horn of Africa that they are not earlier than about 500 A.D. The only cattle in the central Tanzania paintings are very late.

Attempts have been made to date by super-positions of one painting on older paintings—Leakey has, for example, described seventeen phases for the central Tanzanian paintings. Often other archaeologists disagree with the actual number of phases distinguished but nevertheless for several regions a definite sequence exists in which perhaps only one particular phase can be dated.

In East Africa sites are most numerous in Tanzania where upwards of a thousand sites have been discovered. The main concentration lies in the Central Region, particularly in the Kondoa area, though other important clusters occur around

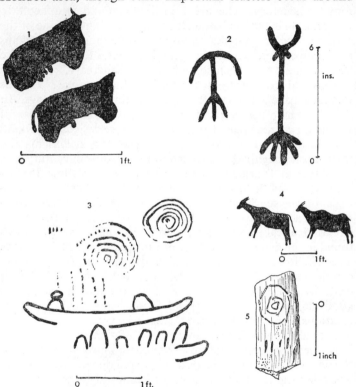

Figure IV Rock painting types in East Africa

1 A cow and bull from Mount Elgon, Kenya (red)   2 Schematic cows from Bwanjai, Bukoba district, Tanzania (red)   3 parts of the frieze at Nyero, Teso district, Uganda, in red showing parts of two canoes and concentric circles   4 Part of the naturalistic frieze from Cheke, Kondoa district, Tanzania showing two eland in red   5 A piece of bone decorated with concentric circles from Nyero rock shelter found in the Wilton Iron Age occupation layer

Singida and Lake Eyasi, the area where the Hadza hunter-food-gatherer peoples still live, and in the western and southern part of Lake Region whilst isolated sites are also found in the south. It is probable that at one time all these clusters formed a single continuum. Except for one site on Mount Elgon and a few scattered sites in Turkana of a very recent period no other paintings have been found in Kenya. In Uganda, sites are confined to the Eastern Region. The majority of the sites occur in and around granite inselbergs and tors where the weathering has created obvious shelters and in shelters along the Rift Valley wall of Tanzania.

In Uganda sixteen sites have been discovered and the paintings are mostly geometric designs, concentric circles, dots and acacia-pod patterns. At two sites, canoes are depicted and it is probable that the art is the work of Late Stone Age hunter-fisherfolk who lived around Lakes Victoria and Kyoga within the last half millennium A.D. Rock paintings have been found on an island in Lake Victoria and some of the symbols shown may be fish of one kind or another. It is possible that the painters in Uganda were similar to the Bushmen since the traditions of the Iteso speak of little yellow folk living amongst the painted rocks before they arrived in the eighteenth century.

In Tanzania the art is largely naturalistic, particularly in Central Region. Figures and scenes occur though single animals and small groups are most common. Many of the paintings are very badly preserved. Animals are most frequently portrayed though there are many lively small groups of people. The earliest paintings are animals painted with a single block of colour, later come outlines with increasing attention to detail. The human figures are found mainly with the later phases. The latest paintings show a degeneration, the outlines being thick and the attitude of the animals stiff. At certain sites geometric designs, some of them similar to those of Uganda, are found amongst the relatively early stages which would suggest that the Tanzanian paintings could be relatively late. The area is still one where underdeveloped hunter-food-gatherers like the Hadza continue with their old forms of subsistence. Many of the more recent human figures are drawn in a most distinctive style with long streaky bodies. The earliest paintings are on the whole the largest and super-positions are found at many of the sites. At many sites the main phases of paintings which are in red, yellows and browns are succeeded by very ill-executed paintings, mostly geometric designs and 'doodles' in white. Similar white paintings are also found in Somalia, Kenya and Uganda and it has sometimes been thought that they are of very recent Iron Age date; how recent we just don't know. In Tanzania certain of the tribes have used the shelters for rain-making ceremonies whilst paintings are still executed at the funeral ceremonies of the Wamia. The Masai of the Rift Valley, who use red ochre for personal adornment often decorate twentieth-century signboards and also rocks with crudely drawn pictures of cows, shields and wild animals.

The paintings in Lake Province are on the whole of a more schematic nature and those at Bwanjai in Bukoba district, where several groups occur, are suggestive of schematic cows which could well be the work of pastoral peoples. At Bwanjai fish are also depicted.

Many of the shelters both in Uganda and Tanganyika are very impressive and the paintings at certain sites such as Mahoho Cave near Isanzu in Tanganyika or Nyero in Uganda are at a height of over ten feet from the floor level of the shelter suggesting the use of scaffolding or at least a climbing-stick, as used in honey-gathering, for their execution.

Also of a late date, though not in all cases necessarily of Iron Age date, are rock gongs. The attention to these prehistoric musical instruments was first drawn by Mr. Bernard Fagg of Nigeria whilst studying the rock paintings at Birnin Kudu in the Central plateau area of Nigeria. Rock gongs consist of a spall or several spalls of rock which have exfoliated off a rock face but are gripped by supporting rocks at one end so that when they are struck they vibrate. They are invariably of granite. Occasionally a rock gong can be a free supported rock (Plate 9). Often along one edge there are signs of intense abrasion where the vibrating or hollow based rock has been struck. Occasionally though, as on Lolui Island, the abrasions are on the face of a large supporting boulder of a tor with the supported rocks acting as a sounding-box. Several rock gongs have been found in Uganda and in southern Africa. The rocks chosen yield anything up to five or six notes. Paintings or engravings have been found in association at several sites in these same areas and also rock slides. It would seem that in some areas the rock gongs and slides are still in use, though often only by children and it seems difficult to know how to date any of the sites. On certain sites the area where the rock

has been repeatedly struck has developed a deep patina suggestive of a certain age. Rock slides in countries where they are
still in use have been associated with fertility cults particularly
in Europe but whether this was their original use in Africa is
impossible to say. It would seem that they must have been
associated with the gongs and paintings as part of magical cults
and whereas the significance of the paintings has long been
appreciated, rock gongs in many areas still have to be intensively sought out and investigated.

PART TWO

The Peopling of Africa and the Foundations of African Society

Many lines of approach have followed to unravel the complicated story of the peopling of Africa during the closing phases of the Later Stone Age and during the Iron Age (2000 B.C.–A.D. 1800). Some, particularly those dealing with differentiating the races of Africa have been discredited. Whilst others, such as those concerned with linguistics, and with the origins of foodstuffs and domestic animals, are being studied intensively. Perhaps more than any other period of Africa's past this is the most fundamental to our understanding of African history and present-day patterns of social development and calls for the widest measure of co-operation between the largest number of disciplines.

Because of the apparent lack of history and the small amount of archaeological research so far undertaken, Africa's past has been over-romanticized on the one hand and underestimated on the other. The few ruins of stone and the oblique references of itinerant Arab scholars and early Portuguese travellers have been magnified into civilization. Hamites and Egyptians have been brought in to account for social systems and cultural progress by some authorities whilst by others the effect of contact has been minimized and the Dark Continent represented as a survival, primitive and prehistoric until the coming of the European. The last chapter in this part is an attempt to study just one area objectively. Many other areas have to be studied in similar detail and with the same detachment before the panoramic view of Africa's past can be justified. The prehistoric foundations of Africa's material culture are tangible but so much that concerns the peoples, their former languages, societies, and their physical form must still remain tantalizingly a series of surmises. Movements of peoples, conquest, inter-marriages, and the extinction of whole tribes have complicated the picture but still a culture history is emerging, though care must be taken to avoid reading too much into the evidence of specialists working in small and often restricted fields.

Towards the close of the Iron Age, archaeology and traditional history are complementary. From the sixteenth century the whole coastline of Africa was known to the outside 'historic' world and in this sense one can speak of a proto-history in that events in the interior are ultimately linked, if only by the receipt of trade goods, with developments outside. In Southern Africa the last fifteen hundred years witnessed folk movements and the spread of ideas of society, government and religion as well as the more material aspects of life. With the crops, cattle, metallurgical techniques and peoples came impulses from the collapsed kingdoms of the Nile Valley. The paucity of the material heritage derived from Africa north of the Sahara is probably a pointer to a similar non-material paucity and it is all too easy to enlarge on the elements of Divine Kingship derived from Egypt, which appear in African Society a thousand years after the fall of the Meroitic civilization, without finding any comparable elements in the material culture.

The Peopling of Africa—The Linguistic and Sociological Evidence

I. THE EARLIER PERIOD

The two major problems in any concise consideration of the peopling of Africa are the spatial vastness of the continent and the time period to be considered. Here we are particularly concerned with the various types of evidence, their quality and how they can be combined. We shall be forced to treat major regions of Africa in terms of the main lines of population movement, pointing to areas and phases of particular significance or of particularly interesting documentation.

As to the time period covered, any line must be arbitrary. But it is worth drawing attention to the fact that between the earlier and the later periods the whole dimension of discourse changes, because the range of relevant evidence is quite different and consequently the scientific disciplines primarily involved are also different. It is not just that archaeologists deal with the past and ethnographers and ethnologists with the present, or rather what they often most misleadingly choose to treat as the present.

The earlier period corresponds largely to the Earlier and Middle Stone Ages, the whole vast period of the development of Man in Africa before the emergence of Late Stone Age and neolithic cultures with their associated peoples and ways of life. This early period covers the best part of the last two million years, if the dating of Leakey's finds be accepted for the moment, whereas, with a few exceptions, the later period covers no more than the last ten thousand and mainly the last five thousand years.

One of the crucial differences is that in the earlier period we are not concerned at all with different races of mankind, but only with different species or sub-species. However much of this may be a relative quibble about words, it is a fact that the present pattern of racial differences in mankind is irrelevant to the earlier period. In this earlier Africa, as in heaven, the differences between Shem, Ham and Japhet; Black, White, Brown and Yellow or Negroid, Caucasoid, Australoid and Mongoloid, have no place. The possibility that certain recent African population groups are genetically linked with the Australoid physical type and the *Pithecanthropus* and *Sinanthropus* forms on the one hand, and that other contemporary races are similarly derived from certain other fossil human and near-human types on the other, is too speculative to require serious consideration by the non-specialist as yet. While Coon still argues for the polygenesis of man, Washburn has recently argued very cogently against it.[1]

If, then, for all present practical purposes, no races can be distinguished in the earlier period, there were also no cultures in the sense of that term to the ethnographer. It is clear that neither flake, blade, nor core cultures, nor even their more refined subdivisions, can possibly have been cultures in the sense of coherent association with specific kinship, economic, political or ritual systems. Even at a later date, the association between Stillbay type 'cultures' and Bushman peoples and their predecessors, and that between Sangoan type 'cultures' and Pygmy peoples and their predecessors, is highly speculative and difficult ever to prove. The reason for this is that human physique and technology are at this level independent variables.

Nothing worthwhile can be said about the distribution of human physical types in Africa throughout most of the earlier period, except that many varied and early types were known in various places, because the archaeological evidence is too sparse, sporadic and fortuitous. The important statement that can be made about the earlier period is that the rich finds of eastern and southern Africa prove that Africa played an important part in the development of early man. Are these finds due to the presence of more archaeologists in eastern and southern Africa than elsewhere, to the better preservation of the remains, or to the fact that this was the only region where these early men lived? Since this question cannot be answered

[1] Washburn, S. L., The Study of Race, *American Anthropologist*, vol. 65 (1963), 3, 1.

nothing useful can be said about the movements of these populations of early men in Africa. But it is perfectly possible that important forms of early man developed, say, in East Africa and spread from there to other parts of the continent and other parts of the world.

Of the later human types, which become relevant as possible direct ancestors of some contemporary African populations, the Boskopoid forms may well have developed in southern Africa and given rise, by many intermediate steps and sometimes in various combinations with other components, to the present and recent Bushman and Hottentot peoples. The Negro peoples of West Africa would appear to represent the most ancient population of *Homo sapiens* not only there but in most of the Sudan Belt from the Ethiopian Highlands to the Atlantic. In the whole of sub-Saharan Africa the Negro, Bushman and Hottentot peoples must be regarded as the most ancient surviving indigenous populations. But the latter two number only a few thousands, while the Negroes constitute the majority population of the whole continent. Caucasoid populations were equally ancient in the North and in East Africa and they may now be represented, with much subsequent admixture, by the Berbers and other pre-Arab populations of Morocco and the Mediterranean coast, the ancient Egyptian element in the modern Egyptian population and the Cushitic-speaking peoples of Ethiopia.

We must now consider the kinds of evidence which can be used to indicate the movements of people in Africa during the later period and up to the present time.

II. TYPES OF EVIDENCE

The study of the biological evidence from human groups has become extremely specialized and cannot be said to have contributed very much lately to our understanding of this part of the subject. Anthropology has also become very specialized, particularly in the British version of Social Anthropology. Studies of the history and movement of peoples had become so cluttered up with misconceptions, wild hypotheses and conjectures a few decades ago, especially in Africa, that reputable social anthropologists virtually abandoned them as a major interest, leaving the weeds to grow so high that they could be cut down and a fresh start be made.

Besides the evidence from human biology, we have to consider the evidence from language, material culture, social organization, custom, and various combinations of all these already composite factors. Thus, oral tradition or ethnohistory is an aspect of language, social organization and custom; ethnobotany is an aspect of language and material culture; archaeology is here primarily an aspect of human biology and material culture with special techniques. Geology, geophysics, climatology and many other specialized studies are of course involved in particular aspects such as dating.

The biological evidence from measurements of hair colour and form, skin colour, cranial and nasal indices and other measures of bodily form, not only now appear both super-racial and subject to very complex causation, but even if this were not so, we have hardly got the beginnings of an adequate collection of field data. The labour involved now appears so colossal that it is difficult to conceive of it being done, especially when enthusiasts in this field are so few. The prodigious efforts of older scholars such as Sir Harry Johnston rightly evoke our admiration. But their lead was little followed and more recent attempts like Oschinsky's[1] show the difficulties of achieving any worthwhile results.

Trevor's study of the Sandawe[2] is excellent of its kind and unique as far as East Africa is concerned. The practical difficulties of achieving an adequate sample have hardly ever been overcome and even if they were the categories to be used in analysis are not established. It is recognized that the adoption of linguistic terms like Bantu, Hamitic and Nilotic as labels for physical groupings is unsound and grossly misleading.[3] But

[1] Oschinsky, L., *The Racial Affinities of the Baganda and other Bantu Tribes of British East Africa*, Heffer (Cambridge, 1954).

[2] Trevor, J. C., The Physical Characters of the Sandawe *J. .A.I.*, 1947, vol. LXXVII, p. 61.

[3] This is particularly true of the term Hamitic, which has no agreed physical or linguistic referent and is a fertile source of misconception. It is most deplorable that these errors should still be perpetuated in what ought to be reliable works, such as Seligman's *Races of Africa* (3rd edition) (Oxford 1957).

Oschinsky's ugly invention of Bantomorph, Hamitomorph and so on has not won general acceptance. In any case, as most physical anthropologists today belong broadly to the medical profession, their interest has turned more to haematological and genetic factors and it is doubtful whether their work will provide any general body of evidence on the peopling of Africa.

A recent study of Sicklaemia in West Africa will be referred to below, and the pioneer work of Lehmann and Raper[1] in Uganda demonstrated a most interesting range of variation. The Hima had a very low sickling rate and the rates of neighbouring Bantu peoples showed a fairly consistent range of variation from low to high in proportion to their degree of contact with the Hima. The forest-dwelling Amba had a very high rate, while the Nilotic peoples fell between this and the Interlacustrine Bantu. Allison[2] pointed out that Sicklaemia is useless as an ethnic-index unless controlled for disturbing selective factors such as its protective qualities in relation to malaria, which are highly pertinent to the varied environment of Uganda. In Livingstone's West African study this factor was included in the argument.

Turning to the linguistic evidence, we can distinguish four kinds of change at the simplest level, that in vocabulary, sound, grammar and meaning. We cannot assume that these four kinds of change follow the same course. They often seem to occur independently, though all can perhaps ultimately be reduced to sound (phonetics) or meaning (semantics) and their combinations in the widest sense.

In the field of material culture, it is hoped that certain items, which can be defined with precision, may provide good evidence on the movement of peoples if they can be linked effectively with the human groups responsible for their distribution. Examples are the xylophone and the sewn plank boat, which are taken as diagnostic of Indonesian influence from the East Coast, or the spread of iron or pottery types or of specific varieties of food crops. With the study of words used for iron, or of maize names, the linguistic evidence is brought in to reinforce that of material culture.

[1] *Uganda Journal*, 1950, vol. 15, pp. 41–42.
[2] *Brit. Med. J.*, 1954, Vol. 1, pp. 290–4.

The most ambitious use of language in this context is the dating technique of glottochronology,[1] which remains controversial in a number of respects, but has clearly given fascinating and important leads which will almost certainly permit more reliable estimates of the age of African languages. The greatest care is required in relating this evidence to the continuous history of social groups, because it is much easier for people to change from one language to another than for a language itself to change.

Then there is what may be called the sociological, the cultural and the ideological evidence. By sociological I mean what can be learnt from a study of the distribution of the very varied forms of social organization, groupings and structure. By the cultural evidence I mean tracing the distribution of specific values, beliefs, practices and taboos from one period to another, while the ideological evidence is that which comes from the subjective feeling of identity which distinguishes one African people from another, and how this relates to tribal names and the names of local and descent groups at all levels. Some supposed tribal names are quite surprisingly modern, or were never recognized by the group in question as the proper name for themselves, but rather were terms of abuse or other kinds of nickname applied to them by their neighbours and hence by foreign travellers, often as a result of a lengthy series of misunderstandings. Other names do stand for some profound identification in the people themselves and are therefore important indicators of population movement and history if their distribution can be traced over a time. But frequently they do not define the limits of a tribe in any accepted sense, but link together a number of peoples wide apart who are usually now considered as separate tribes, or else link together only special categories or strata of population among several different peoples. The East African ethnic terms 'Lwo', 'Lang'o', 'Hima', 'Tusi', 'Iru', 'Hutu', 'Twa', 'Ndorobo' and many others are well-known examples.

Of all these kinds of evidence, the linguistic is very crucial,

[1] Lees, R. B., 'The Basis of Glottochronology', *Language*, XXIX, 1953. Hymes, D. H., 'Lexicostatistics So Far', *Current Anthropology*, January 1960. Armstrong, R. G., 'Glottochronology and African Linguistics', *J. Afr. Hist.*, vol. III, 2, pp. 283–90.

not only because particularly objective evidence comes from
the study of language itself, but because language is so frequently used as a basis for the definition of the groups we are
studying in the absence of anything better. When we say we are
studying the movements of African peoples we obviously beg
the fundamental question of how one 'people' is to be distinguished from another. Whether we use the word people or
tribe in this context makes no difference to the problem of
definition. Tribe is usually held to denote a territorially based
community distinguished by its own language and culture. A
surprising number of groups constantly referred to as tribes
do not meet these criteria. It can be seen again that the relevance and importance of the different kinds of evidence varies
with different levels of time-depth.

Certain major movements of peoples, also certain major
stabilities of peoples, are obviously implicit from a collation
of linguistic and other evidence. Sometimes these movements
and stabilities (non-movements) can at least be seen in sequence
as relatively earlier or later than one another even when dating
is impossible. When we consider 'major movements' it is usually
because there is still too little evidence at such and such an
epoch to consider the minor movements, which are collectively
more important and certainly more meaningful. Therefore
'major' here becomes an unfortunate synonym for 'early' and
for 'large scale'. For what is early there is axiomatically that
much less complete and precise evidence, so it cannot be seen
in any refinement of detail but only in the large scale, where
inconsistencies, inaccuracies and pools of outright ignorance
are blurred, unobtrusive and hard to detect. We hope we see
the wood but are woefully ignorant of the trees.

'Peoples' at this level and in this sense is a rather unsatis-
factory concept. 'Populations' might be better, indicating large
movements under large influences over long periods, of numerous peoples who were unlikely even to be aware of one
another's existence, let alone have any sense of common
identity or unitary structure, whatever similarities we may now
attempt to establish between their physical characters and their
languages, cultures or social organization. These limitations
are rarely frankly stated. At more recent epochs, during the
last millennium and especially the last half of it, it becomes

possible to assess other evidence, including traditions, and to deal with real peoples in the sociological sense. I shall proceed, then, on the basis of this crude distribution between earlier macro-movements and later micro-movements. Of course, there is no implication here of two historical waves, for clearly there was an endless succession of waves, tides, currents, ebbs and flows, of which we see only the very last few and those but imperfectly.

III. WEST AFRICA

It is clear that many of the West African Negro peoples have been near their present habitat for a very long time. Yoruba social systems go back with considerable structural stability of form, whatever the political upheavals and catastrophes, for over a thousand years. Yoruba and Benin tradition, tell of the arrival of politically superior immigrant rulers, as does that of Nupe[1] and of the various pre-Fulani Hausa states. There is no real evidence where high Yoruba culture came from, or indeed that it came from anywhere. In our age when other Africanists are striving to recreate the greatness of Africa, it would be an odd paradox indeed if Yoruba scholars (or Akan, Ibo, Wolof) insisted on deriving their greatness from Egypt, Israel or the Yemen according to taste and proving that it was not really African at all.

It is perfectly possible, though certainly not adequately proved, that there was a cultural continuity from the Nok culture of the Benue Valley to Yoruba, thus indicating a stability and development of about three millennia round the forest fringe of middle Nigeria, moving south in the middle of the period as the forest was penetrated.

It is held likely that the knowledge of ironworking, present in Egypt from the seventh century B.C. and well established at Meroë by about the fourth, may have spread across the Sudan as far as the Nok area within a few centuries after.

Farther west, through the present Dahomey, Togo, Ivory Coast, Liberia, Sierra Leone and Guinea, penetration of the forest by anything more than hunting groups seems to have

[1] Nadel, S. F., *A. Black Byzantium* (Oxford, 1942).

come later, only during the last millennium and little before the middle of it.

In south-eastern Nigeria the Ibo are also an anciently settled population. Cumulative archaeological finds of carved stools and figures indicate a considerable cultural continuity but no firm early dating is possible as yet.

A study of the implications of sicklaemia in West Africa[1] is at least consistent with the view that the Kru-speaking group of peoples, of present-day eastern Liberia and western Ivory Coast, represent the descendants of the ancient, pre-agricultural Negro peoples of a wide portion of the coast, who were later encroached upon by the Mande-speaking peoples from the North, the Akan speakers from the East and the West Atlantic peoples from the West, all these three groups having only been able to penetrate from the Sudan through the forest to the coast with permanent settlement after they were equipped with iron and with suitable forest crops such as the yam.

Murdock credits the western Sudan, near the Upper Niger, with one of the four independent inventions of cultivated plants and agriculture in the world. He regards the 'Nuclear Mande' (Malinke or Mandingo, Soninke, Bambara) as the most likely population responsible and places this revolutionary transformation well over six millennia ago. We have practically no facts of any kind with which to fill in the greater part of this huge period. If this hypothesis holds, this Sudanic agriculture is likely to have reached Egypt five millennia ago, just as the influence of the south-west Asian agricultural complex passed from Egypt to the south and west across the Sudan.

However, Posnansky[2] finds it more plausible to suppose that the idea of agriculture spread from the Middle East, through Egypt, across Africa to the West, and that it caused a secondary agricultural revolution in the western Sudan on the basis of sorghum, bulrush millet, Guinea yams, rice, fonio and sesame.

All the Voltaic[3] and Chadic peoples in the present Upper

---

[1] Livingstone, F. B., 'Anthropological Implications of the Sickle cell Gene Distribution in West Africa,' *American Anthropologist*, vol. 60 (1958,) 3, p. 533.

[2] 'Bantu Genesis', *Uganda Journal*, vol. 25 (1961), 1, p. 86.

[3] e.g. Senufu, Minianka, Bobo, Lobi, Dagomba, Mossi, etc.

Volta, Niger, Nigeria and Chad, as well as the Yoruba, Ibo and
their neighbours, must have received the complex at an early
date and from and by them the agricultural penetration of the
West African forest belt occurred.

It is certainly consistent that the earliest complex society
with state organization known in Negro Africa should have
been ancient Ghana, in the same region of the Upper Niger in
present Mali among the Malinke and Soninke. Its beginnings
lie beyond the dawn of reliable history and by the time of the
first records at the end of the first millennium A.D. it was already
under heavy pressure from northern Berber peoples and soon
after by Arabs. To it the later Mali and Songhai empires from
the thirteenth to the seventeenth centuries were in various
ways successors. However, while documentary evidence has
hitherto focused attention on the ancient Ghana and its successor states, the more recent archaeology tends rather to
indicate the Benue–Yoruba area as the oldest centre of indigenous high culture in West Africa yet known.

The successive empires of Kanem and Bornu, during the last
one and a half millennia represent a blend of stronger eastern
Sudanic influences passing through Kordofan, Darfur and
Wadai from Meroe, Nubia and untimately Egypt to mingle
with those of the Berbers from the north.

The plausible general picture of West Africa, now by far the
most populous part of the whole continent, is of ancient Negro
peoples all along the northern fringe of the forest belt in the
Sudan and spreading far north into the Sahara, with at first
only sparse occupation of the forest and the coast by Negro
hunters and fishermen. This picture would extend from many
millennia B.C. up to the development of agriculture, its spread
from the Sudan through the forest to the coast over several
millennia, the development of elaborate social and political
organization and of high culture in art forms. During the two
most recent millennia we see the culmination of pressure from
the north by Berber peoples, pushing the Negroes southwards,
or perhaps more importantly the central Sahara desiccation
forcing most of the Negroes south and most of the Berber
north, except for the oasis travel and trade routes which continued to link them. During the most recent millennium, Arab
immigration forced the Berbers into islands of the desert and

mountains, itself pressing hard upon the Negroes in cultural influences, religious conversion and miscegenation.

The link between the Negro peoples on the one hand, both physically, linguistically and culturally, and the caucasoid Berbers and Arabs on the other, is quite clear in theory though in practice it became extremely blurred everywhere. The eight million or so Hausa show this blurring, for they are now predominantly Negroes in physique but in language are more allied to the Berbers and other caucasoid peoples. However, the Berbers themselves have acquired a very large amount of Negro blood.

In the eastern Sudan the potent influences were the early Negro culture of Upper Nubia, its relationship to Pharaonic Egypt and the kingdoms of Lower Nubia, its contribution to the Meroitic state and the dispersion of cultural influences from Meroe to the east, south and west after its eclipse by Axum in the fourth century A.D. In Meroitic Nubia itself, this culture was slowly destroyed or incorporated by the Islamic conquest over the next several centuries and, as in the west, the blurred Negro-caucasoid line was pushed considerably farther south than before. By the fourteenth century when the Christian kingdom of Dongola was finally conquered by the Muslims, though it had been greatly weakened and reduced long before, there was a continuous but fluctuating series of Islamic polities stretching from Egypt through Nubia and right across to the western Sudan. The Fur, the Nuba and others remained as isolated remnants of earlier Negro populations surrounded by the Arab sea.

IV. NON-NEGRO PEOPLES IN THE NORTH AND EAST

Through the vast length of eastern Africa, and over an enormous period of time, there are persistent yet very ill-related suggestions of caucasoid peoples. Thus the makers of the Kenya Capsian culture are held to have been caucasoids, perhaps as much as 30,000 years ago. Skulls associated with Kakamas and Magosian Late Stone Age sites in South Africa of about 10,000 years ago are thought to show some connexion. Much later again, Murdock assumes the movement of his caucasoid 'Megalithic Cushites' from Ethiopia into East Africa round about 1000 B.C. He further suggests a movement of some of them to the East African Coast before the arrival of Negroes there. The Megalithic Cushite hypothesis is taken to account for the presence of the Iraqw, Gorowa, Alagwa and Burunge in present-day Tanzania. This cluster of peoples certainly constitutes a mystery worth accounting for. But, though both Murdock and Greenberg call them Cushites, there seems to be no evidence for this. The only expert linguistic evidence is that of Whiteley, who sums it up by saying that some phonetic and grammatical features . . . 'seemed to invite comparison with Hamitic or Semitic languages, but these are inconclusive, and up to the present there is no clear evidence of affinity with any of the large linguistic classificatory groups'.[1] To this one can only add that, if the migration attributed to the 'megalithic Cushites' did occur, there is no evidence that they spoke Cushitic language either. The non-negroid physical qualities of the Bantu-speaking Hima–Tusi and the Nilo–Hamitic pastoralists have also been taken to imply a caucasoid element.

If such caucasoid movements to the south occurred intermittently over a very long period, they did not encounter a vacuum, nor even simple peoples of Bushman type, for it is thought that both the physical forerunners of the Bushmen and the proto-Australoids developed very early in South Africa and may have blended in many different ways. From this developed both the modern Bushmen and the Hottentots, as well as many intermediate forms such as the physically large Bush-Boskopoids thought responsible for Mapungubwe and early Zimbabwe. When the Negroes came, most likely in the shape of the Bantu-speaking peoples, they may thus have blended with and incorporated many such intermediate physical types which are no longer discernible at all as separate entities.

To fill in the general picture of northern Africa, before turning to the southern part of the continent now peopled largely by the Bantu, it is convenient to take focus from Ethiopia. It is known that, through most of the first millennium before Christ, South Arabian influences, later tinged by Hellenistic culture, were penetrating from the Red Sea coast to the northern highlands of Ethiopia, especially through ports such as Adulis, as

[1] Whiteley, W. H., *A Short Description of Item Categories in Iraqw*. (E.A.I.S.R. 1958.)

reflected in the Axumitic state which is known to have flourished from the first century A.D. until the Middle Ages when
the Abyssinian focus of power moved south. From these beginnings, the Amharic peoples have spread their influence from
northern Ethiopia. Physically caucasoid with Negro admixture,
speaking Semitic tongues most closely related to those of the
Arabian peninsular, they combine South Arabian cultural influences with the deeply rooted Coptic Christian tradition from
the pre-Islamic culture of the Sudan and more recent accultur-
ative features from their Cushitic Galla neighbours to the south.

About a millennium ago the Galla and Danakil are thought
to have begun to move down from the Ethiopian highlands, the
former to the south-east, the latter to the north-east, while the
Somali moved due east into the Horn. In their movement to
the south-east the Galla came in contact with the northern
fringes of Bantu settlement, where the latter must already have
incorporated or isolated the previous nomadic Bushmanoid
hunting groups. In the more arid areas favourable to nomadic
pastoralism, the Bantu nowhere challenged the Galla or Somali.
The Somali, however, put increasing pressure on the Galla,
who in turn seem likely to have caused the 'Shungwaya' migration of the Nyika coastal Bantu peoples from what is now
southern Somalia all down the Kenya coast and into Tanzania. Tradition and documentary evidence suggests that this
movement took place in about the fourteenth century. The
Galla pressed so far south as to come in conflict with the Masai
in south-eastern Kenya by the nineteenth century. Somali
pressure seems also to have led long ago to Galla movements
into central and western as well as south-eastern Ethiopia,
while the addition of colonial control at the end of the nineteenth century restricted the Galla to only the central parts of
northern Kenya.

V. THE BANTU-SPEAKING PEOPLES

The face of Africa has been so extensively changed by the
settlement of the peoples who speak Bantu languages, that it
is convenient to focus discussion of the linguistic evidence for
the movements of African peoples round it.

Greenberg's refurbishing of a macroclassification of African languages enjoys great popularity. His inclusion of Bantu in his vast Niger–Congo family carries with it the hypothesis that the Bantu languages were spread by a movement of peoples from the Benue region throughout Africa to the south and east. Guthrie points out that this hypothesis arises largely from the evidence of earlier writers such as Johnston and Westermann who showed that some West African languages had words of possible common origin with Bantu words and that grammatical agreements by prefix, similar to the Bantu concords, were also found in West African languages.

However, Guthrie has accumulated an impressive body of quantitative data which suggests that the area in which Bantu speech developed and from which it spread lay round the Congo–Zambezi watershed.

The non-linguist might well be confused by the wide divergence of expert opinion. While Greenberg's thesis was adumbrated by earlier scholars long before, his striking presentation of it has enabled those in other fields to get a clearer picture of the whole, which, even if inadequately substantiated, has proved a great stimulus to further work which may eventually provide a more reliable as well as coherent basis of classification. On the other hand, Guthrie's work on the whole field of Bantu is unrivalled in detail and extent, yet even here the information which is generally available from it is much too condensed.[1]

Guthrie's analysis, based on the discovery of over 2,300 'starred forms', mostly consisting of stems and radicals with cognates widely spread through numerous Bantu languages, is tested on 200 languages selected for a combination of wide geographical distribution and adequacy of information. This exercise not only reiterates the common basis of all Bantu, but indicates within this, distinct eastern and western ancestor languages. Guthrie suggests that Bantuisms in West African languages are most likely accounted for, not by common origin, but by prehistoric splinter groups speaking a language or languages related to Proto-Bantu having reached West Africa from the south-east and become absorbed.

[1] 'Some Developments in the Prehistory of the Bantu Languages', *J. Afr. Hist.*, vol. III, 2, pp. 273–82. M. Guthrie, 'Bantu Origins: A Tentative New Hypothesis, *Journal of African Languages*, Vol. I, 1, pp. 10 ff.

Remembering that there is no reason to assume that the physique of groups speaking similar languages cannot change, nor that the languages spoken by groups retaining similar physique cannot change, nor that other features of culture and social structure do not change out of step with both physique and language, we may summarize the plausible implications for ethnohistory of this formidable piece of long-term linguistic research. Taking account of Guthrie's linguistic evidence it is possible to surmise that the Negro forerunners of the present Bantu-speaking populations migrated from West Africa to the east along the north side of the equatorial forest belt, thus reaching the Interlacustrine area and proceeding south from there. This movement may well have started some two and a half millennia ago,[1] before the coming of iron, though perhaps in conjunction with the spread of agriculture. Much smaller numbers may have passed more directly south through the Congo forest which was then presumably only sparsely occupied by its ancient pygmy populations, possibly associated with a later phase of the Sangoan culture. Some degree of crossing must have occurred and would have led to paler skin colour than that of the original invading Negroes, as well as other physical modifications. At some point the Negroes who passed through the forest would have made contact with those who passed round to the north, east and south of it. Guthrie's data shows a marked distinction between the Bantu languages of the Congo forest and those to the south of it.

The general evidence from the Interlacustrine area suggests that Negro, and probably Bantu, populations have been there for a millennium or so. Fairly densely settled populations developed, many different superimposed waves of migration occurred and a long process of political elaboration took place. It is perfectly possible that the process of differentiation of Bantu languages could have proceeded a long way during the arrival, settlement, growth, subsequent dispersion, and substitution of populations in the general Interlacustrine area, followed by further migration southwards accompanied by a general fanning out all over the more desirable settlement areas

[1] Greenberg, J. H., 'Africa as a Linguistic Area', in *Continuity and Change in African Cultures*. Ed. Bascom, W. R., and Herskovits, M. J., p. 20.

of southern Africa. This could have led to the situation disclosed by Guthrie in which the populations speaking Bantu languages with the largest number of common elements are *now* to be found in the general area between the headwaters of the Congo and the Zambezi, with extensions to the east and west.

Such a speculative hypothesis tends to reconcile the divergent linguistic arguments of Guthrie and Greenberg, as well as these with the anthropological and archaeological evidence. It is not possible to suppose that the Negroes developed in eastern or southern Africa, where all the evidence consistently suggests that they appeared later than elsewhere. They must have come from the north or the west. Nor is it possible to suppose that the Bantu languages developed among any other than primarily Negro populations. Yet there is nothing to give any plausibility to the idea that Bantu speech developed from any of the language families to the north, that is, the various Sudanic language groups. Linguistic, physical, anthropological and archaeological evidence all force the conclusion of a northwestern origin from West Africa. Nor, despite differences of opinion over detail, is there really any fundamental conflict here between the evidence of Greenberg and Guthrie. Guthrie must be taken as conclusive on the linguistic events of most of the last two millennia. Greenberg's macro-hypothesis refers to a more remote epoch.

VI. THE FINAL PEOPLING OF EAST AFRICA

The final peopling of East Africa, from our present perpsective may therefore be seen as the occupation of the most desirable and vacant areas by the Bantu, mingling with previous occupants, growing in numbers and eventually expanding into all areas except those subsequently penetrated by other non-Bantu immigrants. This is the story of the last two millennia in East Africa.

What kind of blending occurred between the Negroes, with their developing Bantu speech, and the pockets of Bushman hunters and collectors all over East Africa, probably with their various versions of the Stillbay Culture? What blending occurred in the fringe areas of the equatorial forest, which then extended eastward from the Congo right into Uganda, with its sparse pygmy hunting and gathering populations and its Sangoan culture? What happened with the caucasoid makers of the Capsian cultures in the highlands round the Rift Valley in Kenya, and with their possible offshoots who found their way to the coast as the 'Azanians', there to mingle with the various possible arrivals from the Yemen and the Persian Gulf, from Indonesia, China and India, until the Bantu came? Where and when did the blending of caucasoid and boskopoid physical types occur, as implied by various sites both in South Africa and Malawi? What was the impact of the apparently boskopoid creators of the Mapungubwe culture and the Bantu-speaking Negroes who subsequently overwhelmed them? Little more can be said in answer to these and many related questions beyond the fact that this offered ample possibility for the emergence of varied physical types upon the Negro foundation and for even more varied cultures, while the strong Bantu linguistic framework survived and contained all these transformations.

While it is not yet possible to give a coherent account of the complex movements, until the detailed oral tradition of every local group has been collated with all the other evidence, the settlement of the Kikuyu–Kamba cluster and the Chagga–Pare cluster must be seen as part of the first coming of Bantu-speaking Negroes to East Africa. It seems likely that they reached the coast somewhat more than a millennium ago, spreading as far north as the southern part of Somalia, while the reverse movement southwards of the Shungwaya tradition came four or five centuries later, perhaps corresponding approximately with a move inland into the highland forest areas which has continued until the present time, with the Kikuyu still moving into the Kiambu area when the first European travellers reached there in the nineteenth century.

It is likely that the occupation by the Negro agricultural Bantu of the East African highlands, with their caucasoid and bushmanoid inhabitants, was selective. They did not choose the arid plains, which may have passed direct from early caucasoids to later negroid Nilo–Hamites; nor the higher, colder forests, where it was possible for hunters and collectors like the Ndorobo to survive. Hence the present 'island' distribution of contemporary Bantu peoples, such as: the Kikuyu, Embu, Meru and Kamba; the Taita; the Tanzania Meru, Chagga, Pare and Shambaa. The drier plains and grasslands were occupied by successive waves of pastoralists: the Kwavi or Baraguyu, followed by the Masai; the Tatog, Nandi, Kipsigis, Suk, Karamojong, Turkana and all the other Nilo–Hamites.

It is impossible not to think of the age organizations of the East African Bantu and the Nilo–Hamites together, since they form such a distinctive and compact 'culture area' with respect to this one item, despite its manifold variations. Whether in this the Bantu borrowed from the Nilo–Hamites, the Nilo–Hamites from the Bantu, or both from earlier inhabitants such as Murdock's Megalithic Cushites, it is impossible to say with any proof as yet, but the last hypothesis seems as good as either of the other two. The Sonjo may be one of the few remaining examples of the case in which Bantu borrowed from such earlier inhabitants the system of irrigation agriculture which elsewhere has tended to fall into disuse.

The eastern Kamba and the Gogo are examples of Bantu peoples adopting an economic way of life essentially similar to that of the pastoral Nilo–Hamites and so occupying the arid plains which were usually left to the latter. The Tepeth and Teuso of Karamoja District in Uganda may represent the end results of survival by earlier hunters and collectors on mountain tops unsuitable to the later Nilo–Hamites who surrounded them. In central Tanganyika, the Hadza survived as click-speaking hunters and collectors in arid tsetse bush which attracted little competition. The Sandawe likewise survived but eventually adopted cattle-keeping. In eastern Kenya remnants of hunters and collectors like the Boni, Sanye and Langulo survived in symbiosis with invading Galla and Somali.

Only the Teuso, Hadza, Sandawe and perhaps some Ndorobo in Tanzania[1] retained distinctive speech. In the west of the East African region, the Twa in the forests of Kigezi as potters, hunters and jesters to the Tusi of Rwanda, and as fishermen in the dense swamps of Malagarasi in western Tanzania may be final remnants of earlier pygmy populations.

East African Bantuland can also be seen in terms of older

[1] Maguire, R. A. J., 'II-Torobo', *T.N.R.*, vol. 25, 1948, p. 1.

and more recent settlement, corresponding to the most attractive, fertile areas where population grew, economy diversified and complex political systems developed, and unattractive, arid or infertile areas where population was sparse and stagnant technologically, economy remained simple, and political organization was on a very small scale.

In historical depth, population density, economic diversification and political complexity, the Interlacustrine region is by far the most important area of old settlement. With its main points of development in Bunyoro, Buganda and Rwanda, its political orbit of influence included the Nilotic Palwo, Acholi and Alur to the north and the Haya, Zinza and Ha Kingdoms to the south, while the continuous area of political specialization also included the Sukuma, Nyamwezi and, perhaps finally, the Fipa. The main part of this area was clearly one in which the stimulus of one group upon another led to the development of new roles taking the form of political specialization. It was bounded on the north and east by Sudanic, Nilotic and Nilo-Hamitic-speaking peoples of very different social organization, whose presence possibly inhibited the extension of political specialization to the Bantu of the Kavirondo region, and on the south by a radically different balance of land and population.

It is not possible to draw any logical linguistic or cultural line between the Sukuma and Nyamwezi. The important distinction where this is impossible lies between the more open areas of cattle-keeping in the north and the wide expanse of tsetse bush to the south. All over this area hereditary rulers are symbolically designated 'cutters' (*batemi*) of the forest or clearers of the soil. Huge tracts of country were used for nothing but hunting and honey collecting until quite recently, some even till this day. It required a critical combination of population density and political organization to bring such country under permanent or expanding settlement. The larger and better organized the group, the more effectively it could keep the bush clear and the more chance there was of it maintaining cattle to supplement the vagaries of agriculture in a zone of unreliable rainfall. The Sukuma were particularly effective in this and even in recent years have progressively encroached on most of the Zinza country.

South of latitude 4° south there is a vast area sparsely occupied by Nyamwezi and the closely similar Konongo and Kimbu. The Tongwe, Bende, Pimbwe and Rungwa are not as yet very easily distinguishable. Small settlements in high bush are widely separated by large uninhabited tracts. The influence and the organization stemming from major centres like Unyanyembe filtered uncertainly through. In much of this country any settled social organization is both rare and recent. Tiny groups of aboriginal hunters doubtless survived, in mutual ignorance or toleration with sporadic, wandering Bantu hunting parties. It must be remembered that iron remained extremely rare and valuable in many areas of Tanzania and was completely absent or only a very recent arrival in others; Nyamweziland was one of the strongest hinterland centres of Arab influence from the coast directly from the early nineteenth century and perhaps indirectly and intermittently long before. It is almost impossible to extrapolate the results of this on the traditional system with any certainty.

Farther south, in the highlands between Lakes Tanganyika and Nyasa a different form of society with a different history obtains, though there are always intermediate zones and these 'Peoples of the Corridor'[1] are immensely varied in themselves. It is a country of great contrasts, with innumerable remote valleys and mountains where communication was minimal until very recent times. Here, too, many small hunting groups may have survived. But there are also ancient, settled agricultural populations which would appear to have been in this general area for a number of centuries. The ruling families of both the Nyakyusa and Ngonde claim to have come from, or passed through, the Kinga country of the Livingstone Mountains at the north-east corner of Lake Nyasa. The Kinga in turn claim that their rulers came from among the Bena farther east. Indeed, tenuous and indirect ritual links thus connect the Ngonde, Lambya, Fipa, Nyakyusa, Kinga, Pangwa, Bena, Samgu and Hehe over this vast region of south-western Tanganyika, despite many underlying local diversities. The Ngonde[2]

[1] Wilson, M., *Peoples of the Nyasa–Tanganyika Corridor* (Cape Town 1958).

[2] Wilson, Godfrey, 'The Constitution of Ngonde', *Rhodes–Livingstone Institute Papers*, No. 3 (1939).

perhaps developed the earliest; there were signs of increasing
political specialization, though very modest, and from the
sixteenth century onwards they were able to develop a trade in
ivory, probably under indirect Arab influence through contact
along the Lake Nyasa trade routes. These peoples had distinctive systems of socialization, which found striking expression
in the age villages of the Nyakyusa[1] and late marriage complex
of the Kinga.[2]

The Sangu, Hehe and Bena formed a closely interrelated
cluster to the north-east. There were a number of mainly ritual
rulers integrating very small autonomous political entities often
little larger than a village. However, villages were comparatively populous, composed of variants of the large, spacious,
rectangular *tembe* earth-roofed house, which style they share
with the Gogo, Nyaturu, Iramba, Irangi and other Bantu
peoples farther north. Offshoots of ritual lines migrated far
and wide, gradually creating wider solidarities, as in the case
of the Sanga who appear to have passed from Bena to Kinga
country, where they gradually extended their influence and
maintained ritual links with the Nyakyusa. Only in the last
two centuries, when many new forces were playing upon
Tanzania from without, did powerful political rulers appear
among these peoples.

During the second half of the nineteenth century the farthest
ripples of the earlier political upheavals in Zululand reached
Tanzania from the south in the form of the Nguni incursions.
Much of southern and western Tanzania, right up to the
shores of Lake Victoria was intermittently disturbed by them.
While on the move the Nguni bands lived mainly on captured
cattle and food, practising little agriculture. Eventually, however, most of them settled down in many widely dispersed
small groups, contributing a political stimulus but often becoming culturally absorbed to a considerable extent by their
subjects. The largest Nguni polity to emerge from this was in
Songea District in the far south. The mysterious Zimba invasion of the sixteenth century, which passed up the east coast
from Mozambique, sacking Kilwa, slaughtering at Mombasa

[1] Wilson, M., *Good Company* (Oxford, 1951).
[2] Park, G. K., 'The Problem of Late Marriage of Kinga Woman'
(*E.A.I.S.R.* Conference, 1962).

and finally being halted at Malindi by the Segeju, must have been a similar phenomenon, but has left little trace.

The matrilineal belt which extends from the Atlantic coast, all across the Congo, and right through Zambia, Malawi and Mozambique to the Indian Ocean, has a northward extension into Tanzania, through the Yao, Makua and Makonde on the Mozambique border, to the Mwera and Matumbi of the southern Tanzania coast and the Luguru–Kaguru cluster round Morogoro inland from Dar-cs-Salaam. While the Yao, Makua and Makonde have been migrating from Mozambique to Tanganyika in large numbers during recent decades, there is no reason to doubt that some of these matrilineal peoples have been in Tanganyika for many centuries. An important question which arises for investigation is what implications this matrilineal belt has for Guthrie's hypothesis of eastern and western forms of Proto-Bantu.

Further up the coastal stretch between the matrilineal peoples and those of the Shungwaya tradition, whose descent systems are bilateral and in many respects like the Swahili, are peoples such as the Zigua and Bondei who exhibit certain features of both.

Finally, it must be stressed again that the more complete and coherent the story of the movement of peoples in East Africa is made to appear, the more misleadingly it conceals the ambiguity of much of the evidence, the enormous gaps in it and the very great local variation which is found on closer inspection. There is still an almost inexhaustible store of historical evidence to be collected in East Africa, from oral tradition itself, from linguistic study, from archaeology and from the systematic comparative study of social organization and culture. But especially is this truc in Tanzania where the number of traditionally separate groups are fantastically large and rather little reliable and systematic work has been done.

8 The Origins of Agriculture and Iron Working in southern Africa

Agriculture and iron-working transformed Stone Age Africa and provided the material foundations of modern African society. In recent years, as the results of the research of the palaeobotanist have become available to the historian and archaeologist, speculations have been made as to the origins of the staple foodstuffs of Africa. At the present time in southern Africa south of a line drawn from the source of the Niger to the coast of Kenya (Map 2a) the bulk of the inhabitants are Bantu-speaking, agriculturalists (less than 1 per cent. are hunters and food-gatherers) and all use iron. These three common characteristics are to a large extent the product of the last two thousand years and all of them broadly speaking, had contemporaneous origins.

The present agricultural staples of southern Africa hail from three continents: bananas, coco-yams (*colocasia*) and yams from south-east Asia; certain of the millets, wheat and barley from south-west Asia; groundnuts, sweet potatoes, cassava (*manioc*), and maize from the Americas. The last group are all post fifteenth-century introductions following on the discovery of the New World and their importance is only of significance in relatively recent times. In addition, certain crops seem to have had an African origin such as sorghum, pearl or bulrush millet (*pennisetum*) and eleusine (finger millet), fonio (*digitaria*, hungry grass) and certain of the rices (*Oryza glaberrima* in particular).

The biggest problems to decide are—was there an independent origin of agriculture in Africa, when did the non-indigenous crops enter Africa and what was their effect botanically in relation to the local ancestors of the present-day food staples?

The earliest archaeological evidence we have for agriculture in Africa is from the Nile Valley. By about 6000–5000 B.C. agriculture based on emmer wheat and barley of western Asian origin had spread to the middle and lower reaches of the Nile from the Fertile Crescent or the Iranian foothills, where agriculture had first developed around 8000–7000 B.C. Archaeology also indicates that by the fourth millennium B.C. at the latest, as evidenced by such pottery wares as that characterized by 'dotted wavy line' motifs, which is found both at Shaheinab

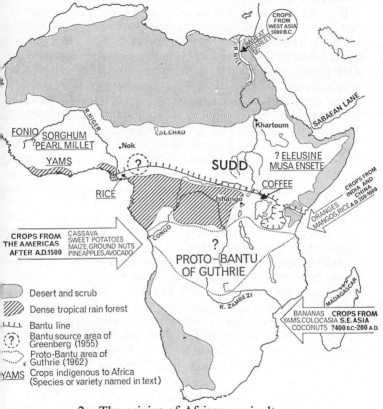

2a. The origins of African agriculture

and at Ennedi, there was regular contact between the middle Nile and the Lake Chad area of the western Sudan, probably by the Ennedi route. Around that period (which equates with Europe's post-glacial optimum) when the climate was rather warmer and moister, it is possible that the Sahara was rather

D

less of a barrier than it is now. If agriculture spread to the western Sudan at that time, Lake Chad and its attendant waterways would have been more permanent and allowed easy movement from the Sudan to the headwaters of the Nile and the Congo tributaries, a factor of great importance in spreading still further afield the new ideas and crops.

It could have been the stimulus of this outside agriculture that led to the development of crops more suited ecologically to the environment of the western Sudan. There is certainly no direct evidence as to the date when crops indigenous to West Africa, such as the wild rices, sorghums and fonio began to be grown, though it is probable that the knowledge of agriculture spread from Nubia and triggered off a local 'neolithic' revolution when food production replaced hunting and collecting. The fact that the wild rices are not cultivated in the same way as the crops obtained from the Nile Valley is an argument in favour of independent invention, though at what date this might have taken place is impossible to say. The area best suited to rice growing, the Niger delta, was not in contact with the influences from the Nile until much later. The Guinea forest yams might have supplemented the diet of the more specialized hunter-food-gatherer, used to prising up roots with his weighted, digging-stick, but it is doubtful if they could have supported widespread and consistently sedentary communities. The techniques involved in cultivating yams were much more a continuation of the methods involved in the food-gathering of the Later Stone Age than original adaptations.

Though it is possible to indicate that certain crops had an African origin in the broad savannah belt of the Sudan or in the highland mass of Ethiopia there is wide disagreement amongst the botanists as to the exact localities of these origins because of the scarcity of the evidence. Nevertheless from the large number of polished and ground stone axes found in Ghana, in the northern region of the Guinea forest belt, it is evident that clearance was beginning to take place and that the population in consequence had increased. However, though clearance was possible by burning and ringing of trees and lopping branches with stone axes, the areas of denser forest and the mangrove swamp of the coastal areas were still a barrier before the advent of iron tools.

Besides the sorghums and eleusine of West Africa or Ethiopia, the crops most suited to more humid and forested areas of Africa were those that had their origin in south-east Asia, the banana, certain of the yams and the coco-yams. These, together with the xylophone, parallel thirds in singing, zithers, methods of tuning musical instruments, the sewn boats, outrigger canoes and various fishing methods form part of a cultural complex introduced to Africa from south-east Asia between 200 B.C. and A.D. 400. On the Island of Madagascar, the Malagache language, though not the bulk of the population, is of Malayo-Polynesian origin. There is as yet no archaeological evidence for this movement.

In East Africa some twenty-one original somatic mutants[1] of the south-east Asian banana have developed and together with the complex nomenclature and present-day usage of the banana in areas around Lake Victoria indicate a long period of development which Simmonds[2] has suggested could be as long as 2,000 years. The differences between the upland East African bananas and those of the East African coast are ascribed to more recent replacement of the older upland variety by new introductions, perhaps dating to the main phase of the Muslim Indian Ocean trade after the ninth century A.D. The banana seems to have spread from the Mozambique coast via the mouth of the Zambezi and the great lakes of East Africa as similar varieties of the cultivated plant and names for the cooked food are found all along this route. The banana is a cultigen and must be planted and carried in the form of suckers and corms as it cannot be grown from seed. Though these corms can survive for short periods they are not the crops of migratory people. Planted crops like the banana and yams depend on successive transplanting. It has also been pointed out by various authorities[3] that the banana need not have come via the Mozambique coast but could have reached East Africa via the Sabaean lane of South Arabia and Ethiopia.

However, if the fructiferous banana came via Ethiopia why

[1] Varieties developing not from cross-fertilization but from the changes taking place in the body cells of the plant itself.

[2] Simmonds, N. W., *Bananas* (London, 1959).

[3] Wainwright, G. A., *Uganda Journal*, vol. 16 (1952), pp. 14–57.

McMaster, D. N., *Journ. Trop. Geography*, vol. 16 (1962), pp. 57–69.

did it not replace as a staple crop the indigenous non-fruiting *Musa ensete* in that area? The Sabaean lane traverses remarkably dry country, but it cannot be entirely ruled out, and this theory is favoured by the fact that from Ethiopia the route impinges directly on the Nile–Congo watershed route which would have facilitated the spread of the banana to both East and West Africa. Again in support of this contention is the prevalent tradition in Buganda that the banana came from the north-east with their first *Kabaka*, Kintu. Until more can be said about the varieties of bananas in Madagascar and India, it will be impossible to resolve the problem of the migration route of the banana but its introduction cannot be later than A.D. 500. It is just possible that the Indonesian influences could also have reached West Africa by sea around the African coast.

We therefore have in Africa to think in terms of two main introductions of agriculture. The first in Neolithic times (or 4000–2000 B.C.) to West Africa of south-west Asian crops which may in its turn have provided the technical knowledge to develop the indigenous African savannah crops; and the second, a much later introduction from south-east Asia via the East Coast of crops suited to the more humid parts of tropical Africa. It is possible that the planted crops reached West Africa at a time when population pressure on savannah land and on the forest edge was becoming felt. If there was a climatic deterioration, as has been claimed by various authorities[1], this would have been taking place in the last millennium B.C. and would have further aggravated the agricultural situation so that crops suited for planting in the forest areas and iron tools, which were then coming into use, would have facilitated expansion.

Besides the crops, we have to consider the evidence of domestic animals. Unfortunately less conclusive research has been conducted on the origin of African livestock and what little work has been done has been concentrated on North Africa whilst in southern Africa it is principally cattle that have been studied. A large part of central and eastern Africa is infested with the tsetse-fly though corridors of land free from them did and presumably always have, existed whilst in the

[1] See in particular, Clark, J. D. in Braidwood, R. J. ed. (1962), *Courses Towards Urban Life*, Viking Fund Publications in *Anthropology*, No. 32.

higher and drier zones considerable pockets of country are suitable for grazing. Nevertheless, pastoralism, except for a minority of the peoples and then mainly in the last half millennium, has been of far less significance than arable agriculture.

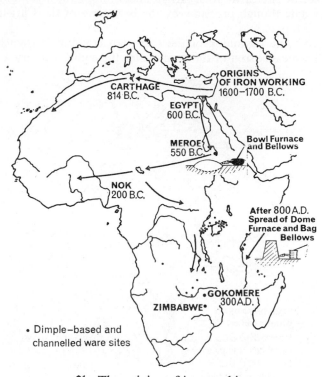

2b. The origins of ironworking

The first definite evidence we have of the existence for cattle in Africa comes from the Nile Valley around 5000–4000 B.C. The longhorn humpless cows (Hamitic Longhorns) of western Asia spread from Egypt through North Africa to West Africa where some still survive. It is probable that this movement was taking place by about 3000–2000 B.C. Other groups of similar cattle occur in the Chad area and may have come directly from the Middle Nile by the Ennedi route whilst others reached the

Horn of Africa. The paintings of the Horn provide illustrations
of long-horned humpless cows of which the Mount Elgon ones
are the southernmost example. Shorthorn humpless cows (*Bos
brachyceros*), again of Asian origin, spread from the north-east
corner of Africa to West Africa and Ethiopia at a somewhat
later date though probably by the beginning of the Christian
era. (Map 2c.)

From the beginning of the Christian era, but particularly
with the expansion of the Arabs after the eighth century A.D.,

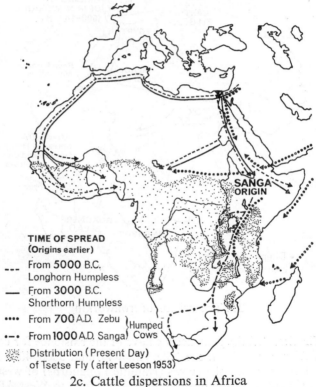

TIME OF SPREAD
(Origins earlier)

- - -   From **5000** B.C.
       Longhorn Humpless

───   From **3000** B.C.
       Shorthorn Humpless

••••   From **700** A.D. Zebu ⎫ Humped
                                  ⎬
•─•   From **1000** A.D. Sanga ⎭ Cows

▒▒▒   Distribution (Present Day)
       of Tsetse Fly (after Leeson 1953)

**SANGA
ORIGIN**

2c. Cattle dispersions in Africa

the Zebu (*Bos indicus*), a shorthorned humped cow, spread
along the East Coast, to the Ethiopian highlands and possibly
also via the Nile–Congo watershed to West Africa. Some of the

earliest finds of domestic mammals from East Africa (Lanet and Nakuru burial site in Kenya) contained bones of this breed. However the main effect of the Zebu was felt in the form of the Sanga, an African cross-bred which originated in the Ethiopian highland area from the hybridization of the humpless cows, mainly of the long-horned variety, and the Zebu. It is probably a variety of the Sanga that is represented on the soapstone bowls of Zimbabwe dating from the fifteenth to seventeenth centuries. The Hottentots, met by the first Dutch settlers at the Cape, had a form of Zebu cow which probably accompanied them sometime in the first half of the present millennium if pottery parallels between East Africa and South Africa are any indication of a folk movement. Evidence of a trickle of peoples from the Horn in the last millennium of the pre-Christian area and in the first of the post-Christian era is available from the Erythriote (or caucasoid) skeletal remains from the Horn, Kenya, Tanzania and Malawi. The long-horned Sanga of the Hima–Tusi peoples most likely accompanied them and cannot be much later or earlier than the first quarter of the second millennium.

Our knowledge of the introduction of iron-working is mostly circumstantial and based partly on deductions from present-day linguistic clues and traditional usage. Iron first appeared in general use in the Nile Valley in the seventh century B.C. Its introduction was a factor in the rise of the Meroitic civilization in the middle Nile Valley north of Khartoum by the fourth century B.C. By the third century B.C. the knowledge had spread to Nok in northern Nigeria, presumably across the Sahara to the Chad region. In the south, one of earliest dates for actual iron-working is of around the third century A.D. from Goko-mere in Southern Rhodesia though finds of channelled ware, normally considered to be the first of the Iron Age wares of Rhodesia, have been dated to around 100 B.C. to A.D. 200 from the Zambesi Valley and Kalambo Falls. It is not inconceivable that an independent knowledge of iron-working might have come from Indonesia which would account for the rather anomalous early date of the Iron Age in the Rhodesias. A well-established Iron Age culture (the Kisalian), in which a knowledge of intricate copper-working and trade was developed, existed in eastern Katanga by the seventh or eighth century

A.D. It is possible, though as yet speculative, that iron spread from the Middle Nile to the Nile–Congo watershed and thence perhaps via the headwaters of the Congo and the Zambezi to Central Africa. Most unfortunately the earliest dates of iron-working in East Africa are not earlier than A.D. 900–1000 and are associated with the final development of the dimple-based wares, which does, however, suggest an earlier date for its introduction. (Map 2b.)

Except for slag and bellow pipes (*tuyères*) little archaeological evidence remains to indicate the origin of the iron-working. The widespread nature of the Bantu stem form *uma* for iron and the present-day use, in the northern part of East Africa at least, of the bowl furnace and bellows, indicate a Sudanic source area. In the coastal regions and large parts of southern Africa the bag bellows and dome furnace of Arabic Indian Ocean origin may have overlaid an earlier use of the Sudanic forms.

Both the origins and spread of iron-working and of crops must be viewed against the suggested origins of the Bantu based on linguistics. Two theories at present prevail, those of Greenberg[1] and Guthrie.[2] Greenberg has postulated a Bantu source in the Cameroons–Nigeria border area whilst Guthrie, though indicating an initial dispersal of 'pre-Bantu' from the Chad area, favours an origin of the proto-Bantu 'somewhere near the centre of the nucleus, in the bush country to the south of the equatorial forest midway between the two coasts' (ca. 7° S.). Oliver and Fage have suggested that the earliest Bantu-speaking peoples may have been hunters and fishermen and moved along the fringes of the Congo forest by the waterways of the Congo and '*encountered and adopted the cultivated plants* of the earliest traders and migrants from south-east Asia'.[3] It is of some significance that amongst the most general Bantu roots were those that concern boats and fishing. Whatever postulate is assumed the expansion of the Bantu was explosive and must inevitably have depended on the availability of crops like the bananas, yams and colocasias suitable for growing in

---

[1] Greenberg, J. H., *Studies in African Linguistic Classification*, Boston (1955).

[2] Guthrie, M., *Journal of African History*, vol. III (1962), pp. 273–82.

[3] Oliver, R. and Fage, J. D., *A short history of Africa* (Pelican), 1962, p. 32.

the less heavily forested regions into which they spread, and on the iron tools which could allow them to clear those forested areas more efficiently and practise some form of slash and burn migratory agriculture.

Physically the Bantu could have emerged from the indigenous Bush–Boskopoid stock of Africa by what the anthropologists term genetic drift, by which is meant the genetic changes taking place in relatively isolated environments. There is no biological evidence from blood grouping or otherwise to suggest that Negro peoples came from outside Africa as was formerly mooted by many scholars. Tobias[1] has concluded from the similarity of the curvature of the occipital bones between the West African Negro and the South African Bantu that they have a close relationship. This similarity cannot be shown to exist with the East African Bantu where greater hybridization has taken place with population elements deriving from north-eastern Africa. The linguistic as well as the evidence of the Erythriote skeletal remains and the early pottery wares of Kenya, such as the Elementeitan, would suggest that there an essentially non-Bushmanoid population element was of pre-Bantu origin. It is possible that the Iraqw[2] and several other small linguistic groups classed as 'Nilo–Hamitic' may have agricultural and pastoral antecedents stretching back to the second millennium B.C. Unfortunately though the stone bowls and cemeteries, like Njoro River cave in Kenya, suggest sedentary life there is little to indicate of what the basis of the economy of these Kenya 'neolithic' communities consisted.

A further unresolved problem concerns the status of the East African ground and polished stone axes. These are particularly numerous in the north-east part of the Congo Republic and overlapping into Uganda. Do these represent Neolithic non-iron-using communities, as their presence would have indicated outside Africa, or could they suggest a people in contact with iron-tool users? The axes and other tools significantly enough are mainly laboriously shaped out of haematite by Stone Age methods. Perhaps they were made by Late Stone Age hunters who used the ironstone in order that their tools

[1] Tobias, P. V., *Zeit. Morph. Anthrop.*, vol. 501 (1959), pp. 9–19.
[2] Wrigley C., *Journal of African History*, vol. III (1962), p. 270.

could possess the same magical powers they assumed the iron tools of the Bantu agriculturalists to have?

What can we conclude about the origins of agriculture and iron-working in East Africa?

Firstly, though agriculture, dependent on wheat and barley and accompanied by long-horn humpless cattle, had spread through the Sudan to West Africa by 3000 B.C. no direct effect was immediately felt in East Africa. In East Africa (in the main confined to the Rift Valley area of Kenya) early cultivators were probably present by 1500–1000 B.C. and originated from the small-scale movement of caucasoid people that had begun in Late Stone Age times. These people had distinctive pottery, burial practices, stone bowls (in the Elmenteitan culture a very fine lithic industry in obsidian), and at Njoro river cave a knowledge of basketry. But we have no evidence as to what their agriculture consisted of or whether they practised a mixed hunting–agricultural economy.

Secondly, some semi-sedentary communities had emerged in Africa before the advent of exotic food crops and the development of certain of the indigenous staples like various of the millets. Whether the vegeculture of the West African forests based on yams and other root crops supported a large population is hard to determine, though at isolated locations where favourable circumstances permitted, such as on the Nile at Khartoum, on the Semliki river at Ishango and possibly around Lake Chad, a certain amount of semi-sedentary settlement supporting large fishing-groups had become established. It is possible that the use of the waterways by these communities, larger than the normal Late Stone Age hunting and food-gathering bands, pioneered and facilitated the eventual movement and spread of the first of the Bantu peoples and of certain of the main food staples and/or a knowledge of iron-working.

Thirdly, by the end of the last millennium B.C. a knowledge of iron-working had spread from the middle Nile Valley to the western Sudan and to the Rhodesias presumably from the same source. The first Iron Age communities were characterized by remarkably similar pottery known as the channelled ware in the Rhodesias and dimple-based ware in East Africa. This cultural homogeneity could be suggestive of a group or groups originally closely linked who spread rapidly over what was in the Late Stone Age relatively thinly populated country. The speed of the establishment of new communities with diversified pottery wares was faster in Central East Africa than in East and by the middle of the first millennium A.D. in areas where native copper and gold was readily available more elaborate cultures, like that of the Kisalian or those of Rhodesia associated with Zimbabwe, were developing.

Fourthly, linguists suggest that the Bantu languages are not much older than 2,000 years. Their speakers spread rapidly from the Nigerian–Cameroons border area or from part of Central Africa in small groups leading to the present-day profusion of related Bantu languages.

Fifthly, around the beginning of the first millennium A.D. the Malayo–Polynesian influence, which resulted in the Malgache population of Madagascar, also resulted in the arrival in eastern Africa of the bananas, colocasias and certain of the yams. These staples were more suitable to much of sub-Saharan Africa than the millets and barley introduced from the Nile Valley. Together with iron tools these crops, in addition to the millets and sorghums indigenous to Africa, allowed population to expand and spread in a significant way. The spread of these iron-using agriculturalists may perhaps be equated with the 'explosion' of the Bantu but no clear evidence is available. It is again likely that this expansion somewhat overlaid the earlier caucasoid movement into East Africa from the Horn of Africa. In much of East Africa the earliest agriculturalists probably lived by a mixed agricultural-hunting-food-gathering economy as their sites are situated around the lakes and along rivers. The various ground stone axes, which are also associated with the Late Stone Age Wilton culture, indicate that some woodland clearance may have been undertaken prior to the ready availability of iron tools.

Sixthly, though livestock could have accompanied the earliest iron users there is no direct evidence of their having done so. The first evidence of cattle consists of Zebu in Kenya and Sanga in Uganda by the middle of the second millennium A.D.

Most unfortunately though increased research on crop varieties by the botanists will be able to clarify the problems of the origins of the various cultivated plants of Africa, and in certain favourable circumstances suggests the possible length of time taken for their 'domestication' and for the evolution of new local varieties, the archaeologist is rarely able to say more than that the community represented by such and such a site was practising an agricultural economy. Except in the Nile Valley where sickles indicate a sown agriculture and where the dry desert conditions often preserve grains of wheat and barley, it is impossible to identify precisely the crops involved. The numerous querns on Iron Age sites suggest millet- or sorghum grinding but few tools survive that can testify to the Indonesian crops, whilst the environmental conditions of sub-Saharan Africa and the very nature of the crops themselves mean that there is no chance of any of them surviving.

Though the distribution-pattern of present-day cultural traits, such as musical instruments, agricultural and iron-working tools, boats, etc. indicates lines of movement, they are often confused or overlaid by later movements, as the Indo-nesian movement was overlaid by the Indian Ocean Muslim influence. The very nature of primitive iron-working which involves the destruction of the furnace to extract the 'bloom' of smelted ore and the aura of mystery in which the art is held, necessitating in many cases the process to be carried out away from the settlement, militates against the archaeologist building up from his excavations a more detailed knowledge of the process of iron-working and its origin in the Early Iron Age.

9 The Problem of 'Sirikwa holes' and the so-called Azanian remains of the Western Highlands of Kenya

Throughout the highlands between the north-eastern corner of Lake Victoria and the Rift Valley the Kalenjin-speaking tribes speak of a previous people—the Sirikwa. The traditions vary concerning the ethnic and economic background of the Sirikwa and on what has become of them, but they are important to the archaeologist since numerous features of the landscape are attributed to them. These, especially the hollows called 'Sirikwa holes' by the local peoples, can confidently be dated beyond living memory; and, if they were not made by Kalenjin peoples themselves, must attest considerable changes in their customs and economy. However, while it is not suggested that the traditions are wholly unhistorical, in view of their inconsistencies it is dangerous to accept blindly for any archaeological remain a Sirikwa origin: the word cloaks a considerable element of doubt.

Moreover, though some of these features may prove to be connected with or developed from one another, there is little ground for assuming that all belong to a single culture, or to an 'Azanian civilization', which Huntingford in 1933 claimed had covered large parts of Kenya and northern Tanzania some centuries ago. The evidence for the existence, extent and dating of this 'civilization' rests upon some very tenuous and inadequately quoted oral traditions and the dubious assumption that various archaeological remains in different regions, some of them very cursorily described, ought to be linked. Some general works on African history have developed Huntingford's theme. Davidson tries to trace 'Azanian' works and influence all down the eastern side of Africa, whilst Murdock, using some more original arguments, speaks of 'Megalithic Cushites' in the East African highlands. In particular both writers place undue emphasis on reports of graded roads, agri-cultural terraces and irrigation works, and the latter on menhirs.

The following notes are intended as a brief account of the features variously attributed to the Sirikwa, 'Azanians' and 'Megalithic Cushites', their general distribution in the western highlands, and the problems they pose. Descriptions of most have appeared in several publications, particularly by Hunting-ford. A number of these sites have been dug into, but careful and complete excavations have been very few. More will be necessary before their various dates, purposes and cultural backgrounds, and their place in the wider context of African history can be firmly established.

Though the name 'Sirikwa hole' is not entirely satisfactory, it is widely known and hence retained here, since to speak merely of 'hollows' or 'saucer-shaped depressions' is too vague, while the names 'hut-circle' and 'pit-dwelling' are misleading and not necessarily justified by the present evidence. In groups of between half a dozen and a hundred or more they are a common feature of the hill-sides of Kipsigis, Nandi, Uasin Gishu and the high country of Elgeyo and Marakwet. In some flatter parts of western Uasin Gishu and Trans-Nzoia they are rare, but they occur beyond on the forested slopes of Elgon. In fact they have been reported from almost all the highland districts either side of the Rift. The work of erosion, vegetation and in many cases animals or agriculture often leaves their details and measurements poorly defined: however, they are generally between 25 and 60 feet in diameter and, depending on the slope, up to 12 feet deep. They are excavated from the hill-side and the upcast is commonly banked up to form walls on either side of the downhill-facing entrance. Where stone is available, as in northern Nandi and Uasin Gishu, it is often employed for the walls. Sometimes stones are roughly piled with earth, but some well-preserved examples contain neatly coursed dry stonework lining the whole interior. Small annexes at a raised level at the side and back have been reported. These seem rare and to occur only with stonework; natural erosion, accentuated perhaps by cattle or goats, can give the impression of an annexe. Mounds, broad but rarely more than 5 feet high, are not uncommon close by or directly below the entrance.

The Nandi and other Kalenjin people regard these hollows

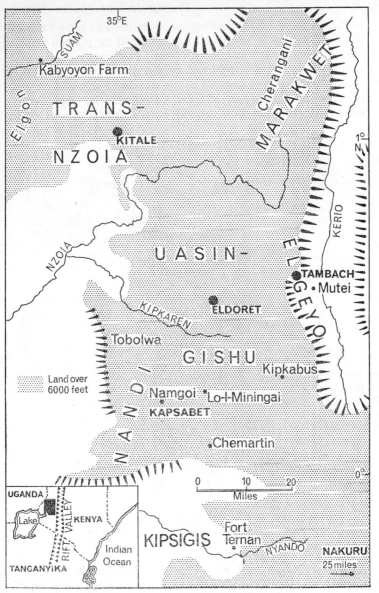

3. The Western Highlands of Kenya

as the cattle-*bomas* of the Sirikwa or perhaps in some cases of
the Uasin Gishu Masai, who once occupied the plateau named
after them and parts of eastern Nandi. That they housed cattle
rather than men is supported by the tea-planters in south-
eastern Nandi who complain of the alkaline soil in and around
them believed to be derived from keeping cattle. One recently
excavated at Namgoi in central Nandi produced very little

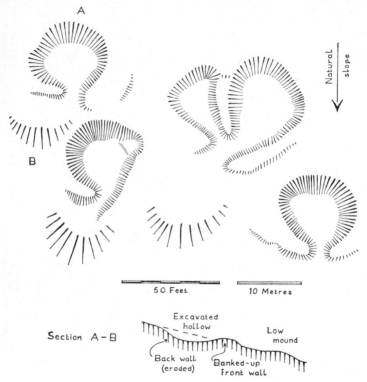

Figure V Plans of stone structures and 'Sirikwa holes'
in the Western Highlands of Kenya

domestic rubbish and no definite hearth, while a section
through the mound outside the entrance revealed a deposit of
what looks to be animal dung scooped out of the hollow. A

sample of this awaits chemical investigation. Wall daub, however, preserved as burnt clay showing the impressions of wattle, not previously recorded from this type of site, suggests that human occupation was at least intended. Moreover in various places pottery and other domestic remains have come to light in or close to 'Sirikwa holes', and Huntingford records a hearth in one in the Kipkaren Valley in northern Nandi. Others excavated near Nakuru outside the region covered here- two with an adjacent mound by M. D. Leakey at the 'north-east village' on Hyrax Hill, and one by Posnansky at Lanet- produced definite evidence of human occupation; so also did one of a very big group of large 'Sirikwa holes' of an apparently variant type recently excavated by Susannah Chapman at Kabyoyon Farm on the Uganda side of the Suam at the north-eastern foot of Elgon.

It seems therefore that most 'Sirikwa holes' represent house-sites, but this need not preclude the keeping of stock under the same roof. A homestead may have consisted of two or more 'holes' with different purposes assigned to each, but this could be confirmed only by extensive digging. The excavation at Kabyoyon Farm, however, revealed within the large hollow (and structually independent of it) two contiguous round huts 12 feet across, attested by slots for beams or posts. But other excavations have failed to discover slots or post-holes, thus making considerations of building type conjectural: flat-roofed houses (*tembes*) like those now used by the Iraqw and other tribes in northern Tanzania have been surmised.

The abundance of 'Sirikwa holes' and the size of some groups (Huntingford's 'pit-villages') have promoted the view that this region once possessed a very dense population. Were all occupied at one and the same time this might indeed be so, but it is clear that they are often successive. It is not rare to find later hollows blocking the entrance or even cutting through the walls of earlier ones, and a new wall built through the middle. Some examples of this have formerly been misinterpreted as double 'Sirikwa holes' containing a central partition.

Huts do not last many years, and when building a new one it was doubtless simpler, especially if stock had been housed, to dig anew. Large groups would appear therefore to attest the continued occupation of a slope over a considerable period by possibly no more than a single family.

Very little iron has been recovered from the excavations mentioned here: nevertheless that 'Sirikwa holes' belong to the Iron Age seems a safe assumption in view of the frequent occurrence of iron slag and pieces of tuyères apparently associated with them, the paucity of stone artefacts, the evidence of the traditions suggesting no great antiquity, and the pottery both from surface collections and excavations. Characteristics of this pottery are a 'sandpaper' finish, gourd-like shapes with straightish or reverted rims, handles, spouts, and rouletted-cord decoration. In several respects these characteristics have links with the present-day pottery. It is not yet possible to offer a tentative pottery sequence: but everted rims which look to belong to modern globular water-jars do not apparently occur in association with spouts, while spouts are nowadays unknown. 'Sirikwa holes' containing spouts are likely therefore to prove fairly early; those with everted rims late. The pottery from the Iron-Age occupation of Site I at Hyrax Hill must belong somewhere in this sequence. The Lanet excavations provide a possible indication of the date of the earlier period. Spouts were found in the hollow, while charcoal from beneath the bank of the nearby earthwork has been dated by the radio-carbon method to the late sixteenth century A.D. However the contemporaneity of the two features remains unproven, and it would be unwise to rely on a single dating. It is hoped that in time, by plotting the distribution of various characteristics of the pottery and other finds and of different structural methods of the 'Sirikwa holes' themselves, information will be obtained on the spread and development of 'Sirikwa holes' and the culture to which they belong.

It has been suggested that the stone houses around Tambach on the Elgeyo escarpment and in certain parts of Uasin Gishu are derived from 'Sirikwa holes'. One at Tambach, consisting of two adjoining rooms and a curving entrance-passage, and inhabited by Elgeyo in the 1930s, is well described by Galloway,[1] and other overgrown examples, including one recently cleared and excavated, are essentially identical. They are slightly

[1] Galloway, A., 'Stone Structures on the Uasin Gishu Plateau', *South Afr. J. Sci.*, Vol. XXXII (1935), pp. 656–68.

sunken and the internal revetment walling is similar to that of the best stone-lined 'Sirikwa holes', but the house-plan shows little connexion. None of the stone houses looks very old and pottery from the one excavated is similar to that now used by the Elgeyo, though the recent occupation of some of them does not in itself date the stonework or the origin of this type of house. There is some uncertainty on whether this should be attributed to the Elgeyo or the 'Sirikwa'.

Stone enclosures in parts of eastern Nandi and Uasin Gishu, including areas from which 'Sirikwa holes' appear to be absent, may be an adaptation to flatter and in some cases extremely rocky ground. Up to ten may be found fairly close or scattered over a small area. Most are roughly circular or oval, but some very irregular. Variations of between 25 and 70 feet have been noted in the longer measurement. The walls are up to five feet high consisting of neatly piled rather than built stonework, essentially free-standing, not revetting. Presumably they were surmounted by fences. Entrances, where preserved, are about two feet wide and sometimes marked by upright stones, but roofed passages are also reported. In some cases the wall is continuous and a gap could have occurred in the fence only. The interior is commonly slightly hollowed, while a raised circle in one example showed that it had contained a hut. Though large trees have had time to grow in many enclosures, the state of the stonework suggests that they have not been abandoned very long.

Evidence of former agricultural practices is not widespread. *Stone-wall terracing*, both to clear the ground and to hold the soil, is practised on parts of the Elgeyo escarpment and to a lesser extent in the Kerio Valley and the Tuken hills beyond. Though known to predate the recent efforts to introduce hillside terracing to prevent erosion in many parts of Kenya, its origin is obscure. Some terraces are under thick bush, but this grows quickly on fallow fields. A cutting was made through a series, said to have been abandoned about eight years ago, adjacent to the stone house excavated at Tambach. An earlier series of walls was discovered buried by later soil. It could not be established whether these were contemporary with the occupation of the house, but again modern types of pottery were found.

Though the original and best engineered of the Marakwet *irrigation furrows*[1] were by tradition made by a previous people, there is nothing definite to connect them with any other feature mentioned here. At Mutei in the Elgeyo part of the Kerio Valley similar but more poorly executed furrows are led off the Torok, and there is a dilapidated stone and earth dam, presumably once fed by a furrow.

The irrigation canals reported in central Nandi appear to be no longer maintained.

Also worthy of mention are some intricate systems of channelling water from springs on the slope of a small valley near Kipkabus in southern Uasin Gishu. The channels are about three feet wide and up to two feet deep with stone-built sides recalling the entrance-passages to the Tambach stone houses. Their purpose must have been to maintain a supply of water for cattle in the valley. They have been disused for 50 years at least, and may possibly be connected with a group of 'Sirikwa holes' of which some contain stonework a short distance above.

Hollow-ways, apparently cattle or sometimes elephant tracks of indeterminate age, are not uncommon, but the dykes and stretches of ancient roads which Huntingford records seem to be mostly destroyed.

Frequent in the region are groups of cairns, obviously graves, often numbering fifty or more, in areas where rock is available. This is normally *lava*, but *schist* is used in a group in Cherangani. They measure 20 to 60 feet across and up to 13 feet high, though few reach half this height. Almost always they are on sloping ground and their shape hence suffers from slip, despite a ring of big stones commonly delimiting the base. They are built of piled stones of various sizes without earth, though many are much covered with wind-blown earth or leaf-mould and hence vegetation too. A subsidence in the top of some cairns (one near Eldoret has three) raises the possibility of collapsed wooden structures underneath.

In dismantling one at Chemartin in south-eastern Nandi it was seen that the cairn had been built around the centre where there had probably been a cavity. But there were no finds, save two secondarily worked flakes of obsidian among the top

[1] Hennings, R. O., *African Morning* (1951), describes the irrigation works in an autobiographical account of the Elgeyo region.

stones. The acidic soil may be responsible for the failure to find any trace of a burial. Similarly in two cairns opened on Cherangani cavities were reported but containing only charcoal. However, from another at Fort Ternan in northern Kipsigis, stone pestles besides human, antelope and rodent bones were recovered.

Occasionally groups of cairns exist side by side with 'Sirikwa holes', and it is hoped to excavate on one or more such sites. At present, however, there is nothing to show that this juxtaposition is significant or that the cairns are of Iron-Age date. Their distribution accords fairly well with the former territory and raiding country of the Uasin Gishu Masai, and some very uncertain traditions ascribe those at and near Lominingai in eastern Nandi to the inter-Masai wars of the nineteenth century. The Uasin Gishu have now vanished, but present-day Masai practice argues against such an origin for these cairns.

Presumably they must in some way be connected with other types of cairns described from various parts of East Africa. Further the practice of burial under small piles of stones sometimes within a house is not entirely unknown among the Kalenjin tribes, and small cairns up to two feet high and ten feet across sometimes occur in or by stone enclosures and in at least two of the stone houses at Tambach. But it is unlikely that these bear any direct relation to the groups of larger cairns.

Though ant-hills are common, no man-made *earthen mounds* have been noticed, other than those mentioned above connected with 'Sirikwa holes'. Most, if not all, of those recorded by Huntingford have been levelled.

Lastly, on *megalithic structures* it is best to quote Huntingford.[1] 'No megalithic structures have been seen, except the debated monument at Tobolwa (above the west Nandi escarpment) and a curious circle of stones at the foot of Kaptepe hill' (a rocky eminence in northern Nandi). The first in its present state it would be pointless to debate further; of the second nothing more is known.

[1] *Nandi Work and Culture*, H.M.S.O., London pp. 6–11 (1950)

PART THREE

The History and Archaeology of the East African Coast

The East African seaboard was relatively unexplored archaeologically until the work of Mr. Kirkman at Gedi in Kenya and of Mr. Chittick at Kilwa and countless other sites in Tanzania after 1948. Quiloa and Melinde appeared on late medieval maps and the story of the conquests of the Portuguese and even of the medieval Muslim Sultans was known to the historians. But it was all a study exotic to the hinterland of Africa. As excavation season succeeds excavation season both on the coast and in the interior it is obvious that though the contact was slight the influence of the coast was important. Beads, cowrie shells and cotton cloth in interior Buganda attest by the seventeenth and eighteenth centuries the influence of the coast just as much as many of the lesser food staples like citrus fruits, methods of iron-working and isolated elements of language. Further back in time before the influence of the Arab there still remains undiscovered the impact of the Indonesian cultural elements so important to the story of Iron-Age Africa. Kilwa, acting as the entrepôt for the gold of the Empire of Mwenemutapa traded from the mines of what is now Rhodesia, through Sofala on the Mozambique Coast, had an indirect connexion to Zimbabwe and the other ruins south of the Zambezi.

The same porcelain, though in small quantities, is found in Rhodesia as on the coastal sites. Visited by dauntless Arab scholars, the coast provides an essential link with the world outside, a world of written documents, of well-organized intercontinental trade, in the mainstream of human history. The impact of trade on societies otherwise untouched by outside influences will never be known though the speed by which tobacco-and pipe-smoking in the seventeenth century, to quote only one example, spread through the heart of Africa is some indication of the unseen processes involved.

10 The history of the coast of East Africa up to 1700

The early history of the coast of East Africa, that is almost until the thirteenth or fourteenth century A.D. is virtually unknown and what can be said is still largely a matter of conjecture, or, to be polite, inspired interpretation. If we are ever to get beyond this stage, it will be by archaeological excavation of sites, whose existence has not been proved, although it is possible to hazard a guess as to where some of them may be.

The original population consisted of people of Bushman type whose implements have been found in many places on the coast of East Africa. Subsequently, at times unknown, the principal components of the present coastal population arrived—the Galla, the Somali, the Bantu and the Arabs.

The Galla were a Hamitic people, that is they were related linguistically to the Arabs. They came across the Red Sea from south Arabia, certainly as early as the beginning of the first millennium before Christ. They occupied the whole of the north of Somalia, but were subsequently pushed south and west by the Somali. In the sixteenth century they overran southern Ethiopia, and most of the coast of Kenya to a few miles north of Mombasa. In the nineteenth century the coastal Galla were in decline and, attacked by the Masai and the Somali, they withdrew northwards. The final blow came in the sixties, when their chiefs were treacherously murdered by the Somali and the whole coastal group practically liquidated. They had remained a nomadic pastoral people and their impact on the coastal civilization was purely destructive.

The Somali were a branch of the Hamite stock who had followed the Galla and settled along the southern shores of the Gulf of Aden, perhaps during the first millennium before Christ. Unlike the Galla they responded to foreign influences, and perhaps as early as the tenth century began to accept both Arab blood and Islam with enthusiasm. At the beginning of the second millennium A.D. they were driving the Galla southwards and westwards and dominating the Bantu agriculturalists of the Webbe Shebeli. Their influence on the Arab cities of the Benadir, Mogadishu, Merca and Barawa, developed from a trading partnership to a political domination. This was more or less acceptable to the Arab immigrants because of the possession of common interests and a common religion.

The arrival on the coast of the Bantu from the interior has been put to the middle of the first millennium A.D. At their farthest northern extension they reached the Webbe Shebeli but were subsequently—probably about the eleventh century—driven south by the Somali to the valley of the Juba, where they remained for another five hundred years. In the sixteenth century, they were driven south again by the Galla, but in the later nineteenth century recovered some of the area they had lost. Their present northern limit may be said to be the River Tana in Kenya. How they came to the coast is also a matter of argument. One view is that they first reached the coast in the south, coming down the rivers of Portuguese East Africa, then moved north along the coastal plain; another is that they came down the northern rivers as well, the Juba, the Tana, the Sabaki and the Ruvuma. Both may be right, though the greater number probably came up from the south.

The first Arabs to reach the coast probably arrived in some places before the Bantu, though no communities are likely to go back to such an early period. They came from the Yemen and from the Hadhramaut, and their interest in East Africa was an extension of their old established trade in the Gulf of Aden. Unlike the other peoples of the coast they had a tradition of urban life and a familiarity with the complexities of trade and politics. However, they were not immigrants, but came and went as traders without capital commitments, obligations or ambitions except to make money.

The coast of East Africa towards the end of the last millennium B.C. was brought into the Asian commercial system, to provide raw materials and curiosities for the more sophisticated countries across the sea. The commodities which first attracted the outside world of Africa were aromatic gums, ivory, slaves, tortoiseshell, leopard skins, rhinoceros horn, gold, and the more prosaic hides, palm oil, cotton, copper and iron. Some of these, such as ivory and rhinoceros horn are mentioned in the earliest accounts of the trade and have survived nearly two thousand years of exploitation. Curiously enough, the one old-established manufacture, a coarse cotton cloth, died out in the nineteenth century in face of the competition of mechanized industries of India and America.

For payment were brought spears, knives, axes, cloth, and later beads and porcelain. For a long time the goods supplied had little relation in value to the goods obtained, even considering the dangers to person and capital involved in getting to Africa and back again. The shrewd Captain Guillain in the early nineteenth century even remarked that the goods brought were of trifling value in order to keep the prices down and the profit high. This may well have been the case, though goods of greater value would not have been much appreciated. The Africans would have preferred the useful metal, iron, to gold, and a good spear to the most exquisite work of Chinese craftsmanship; the Swahili upper class, a heavy celadon dish to a bowl of egg-shell porcelain.

The earliest account of the East African trade is in the well-known *Periplus of the Erythraean Sea*, which is a trader's handbook to the commerce of the Indian Ocean, written in the first or early third century A.D. by an Alexandrian Greek. The Alexandrian Greeks played a minor part in the trade but it is characteristic of the inquiring spirit of the Greeks that it should have been written by one of them. The principal actors were the Arab merchants of the Yemen and their Hindu counterparts from Gujarat. The trade was centred on the markets of south Arabia and the south shore of the Gulf of Aden. It revolved around the trade in aromatic gums from the Hadhramaut destined for markets to the north, the frankincense country *par excellence* and from Somalia, the land of myrrh, as later trade was to revolve around the gold of what is now Rhodesia. It was by no means bilateral. The Hindu merchants arrived to exchange their more precious products, particularly cinnamon and the renowned Indian swords, with their Graeco-Egyptian colleagues.

It is possible that this branch of the trade was more important than the other, since the Indian merchants were not allowed to go farther up the Red Sea than the port of Ocelis, which has been located on the coast of Yemen opposite Perim Island. The great market at this time was the inhospitable headland of Hafun fifty miles south of Guardafui, one of the most promising sites for archaeological excavation on the coast of Africa. I would like to commend it to some enterprising and well-endowed archaeologist—it would cost a lot of money to operate in this area.

The trade goods were glass, cloth, copper and brass, both in sheet form and made up into articles, silver plate, small axes,

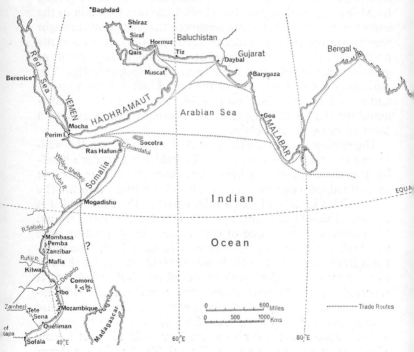

4. The Indian Ocean showing medieval trading ports

adzes, swords, ghee and wheat. It is interesting that cloth and textiles came from both India and Egypt and no doubt went both ways. English shoes are as popular in Italy as Italian shoes in England. The whole report, both in the details and in the treatment, has a remarkable contemporary flavour. The facts of honest trade are as permanent as the facts of nature until other factors are allowed to intrude.

The mention of palm oil as an export of Africa indicates that the Indian connexion is an old-established factor, since the coconut tree is probably of Indian origin and could only have been introduced by some enterprising traders. There were two Indian areas concerned with the trade. The northern, was on the coast of Gujarat and Baluchistan, and the southern, the Malabar coast, the present Travancore.

The picture it gives is of a state of affairs that might be called speculative but, for the stretch of the coast down to the middle of the present Tanganyika no longer exploratory. Conditions might be primitive, the chances fifty-fifty, but the risks were known and could be calculated. There is a refreshing absence of marvels and mysteries. Nothing as good or as factual was to be written until the days of Captain Guillain in the middle of the nineteenth century. It is, however, a trader's handbook— how to make money in the Indian Ocean—and only touches on political affairs when they are sufficiently organized to affect this operation.

The African trade of the *Periplus* is mainly concerned with the Gulf of Aden. The coast of East Africa, properly called Azania, and its trade is mentioned as an extension and not as an independent area. Anchorages along the Benadir coast—the area between Mogadishu and Kismayu and a group of islands approached by a channel—are mentioned by Greek names which have now disappeared. However, one of the anchorages, Serapion, appears to be Warsheikh, and the Pyralaon Islands to be the Lamu Archipelago. Three days beyond, there was the island of Menouthias, perhaps Zanzibar, and then the famous Rhapta, called after the sewn boats, the Swahili *mtepe*, which may be in the area of Kisiju south of Dar-es Salaam, where an allegedly Roman bead was found a few years ago.

This was the extension of Azania which was known as the Ausanitic Coast but is nevertheless considered by the *Periplus* as part of the same commercial area. In the words of the *Periplus*:

There are imported into these markets the lances made at Muza (which is the port of Mocha) especially for this trade, and hatchets and daggers and awls, and various kinds of glass; and at some places a little wine and wheat, not for trade but to serve for getting the goodwill of the savages. There are exported from these places a great quantity of ivory, but inferior to that of Adulis, and rhinocerous-horn and tortoiseshell (which is in best demand after that from India) and a little palm oil.

This is an admirable concise consular report. We shall have to wait over a thousand years before anything approaching it is available. It is as valuable, however, for what it omits as for what it states. There is no mention of slaves, though of course they are referred to in connexion with Azania proper. Culturally it is equally explicit and concise:

Along the coast live men of piratical habits, very great of stature and under separate chiefs for each place. The Mepharitic chief governs it under some right that subjects it to the sovereignty of the state that is become first in Arabia. And the people of Muza now hold it under his authority, and send thither many large ships using Arab captains and agents, who are familiar with the natives and intermarry with them and who know the whole coast and understand the language.

The tall men of piratical habits may be South Arabians, or the Malays who were going to form the Malagasy race. There is nothing to suggest that any of the later coastal peoples could be described in these terms.

Further, the author mentions the intermarriage of the Arab captains with the natives, implying that there were other natives more tractable. Already there was the later set-up of town and country—one semi-foreign, renegade, expatriate, as you will; the other pure, untamed, barbarous. An Afro–Arab racial pattern of the coast was in existence in the first century A.D. However, there is not necessarily any connexion between the Afro–Arabs of the third and ninth centuries. There may have been a complete break.

Finally, there is the recognized authority of the Mepharitic chiefs under the overall government of the Himyarites. The Mepharitic chief is mentioned as living at Saua (possibly Tais) about forty miles from Mocha. He in turn had farmed it out, very sensibly, to the merchants of Mocha who were the people to be affected by it. This granting of authority to a body of merchants is, I think, confirmation of my view that government in this case consisted merely of jurisdiction over the merchants so that the worst excesses of trade competition could be moderated. It was a personal, one might say consular, not a territorial authority. In fact, until the establishment of colonial authorities in the nineteenth century, there was nothing that could be called administration, even in the medieval sense of the word, on the coast of East Africa. When, therefore, we talk of the history of the coast we must put aside all thoughts of political history such as we know from the countries of Europe, Asia, and later America. The history of the coast is a history of markets, towns and to some extent individuals. Behind the towns were the tribes, varying in size and cohesion, clans and even communities of individuals, living in a sometimes happy anarchy. For this period our sole source of knowledge will be from archaeological excavations.

The *Periplus* had no successor, and the coast disappears from knowledge for six to eight hundred years. The Indian trade of course went on, and in fact seems to have struck a new peak during the 'Indian Summer' of the Roman Empire, which filled the first half of the fourth century, but this may not be true of the East African trade. However, the state of the coast was not uneventful, for this is the period of the Indonesian settlement of the Comoros and Madagascar, one of the most extraordinary migrations in the history of man. No traces of the settlements which one would expect to have existed on the mainland have yet been found.

The birth of Islam and the civil wars over the Khalifate had a great effect on the development of the coast of East Africa. The political or religious malcontents found new homes across the seas, as was to happen a thousand years later in America, with Europe bitterly divided between Catholics and Protestants. It is possible that this new interest was a complete refoundation, not a renewal of existing links, although the greeting given to the Arabs by the inhabitants of Sofala in the twelfth century, 'Welcome sons of the Yemen', is perhaps evidence that the overseas trade never completely ceased.

The next gleam of illumination comes in the geography of Masudi, who visited the coast at the beginning of the tenth century. The authority of the Mepharitic chief has disappeared. Masudi sailed to an unidentified island known as Kanbalu, which I once thought was Ras Mkumbuu in Pemba but is probably one of the Comoros. He sailed from Sohar in Oman in a ship of Siraf, a port on the Persian side of the Persian Gulf, and the trade was now in the hands of the eastern Arabs. At Kanbalu he found a Muslim people speaking the language of the Zenj—presumably a form of Swahili. He mentions no other settlements, though it seems most unlikely that none were in existence. Masudi also mentions Sofala, the land of gold, and a King of the Zenj who had cavalry that went to war on bullocks.

Masudi dated the colonization of Kanbalu to the time of the conquest of Cyprus by the Arabs, which would be about the middle of the eighth century. We also have a number of traditions, some recorded by the Portuguese in the early sixteenth century, from a history of Kilwa, others in a history of Lamu, compiled in the late nineteenth, both recording early Arab migrations from Arabia and Persia to East Africa. The most significant of these is the story of the arrival of the 'Emozaydij', the followers of Zaid, the grandson of Hussein who fled from persecution in Arabia in the seventh century and founded the first settlements on the coast at places where they could defend themselves. They were followed by other political refugees from Oman, who had been driven from their native land by the iron governor of Iraq, Hajjaj ibn Yusuf. Finally, there is the story of the foundation of Kilwa by fugitives from Shiraz at the end of the tenth century. None of these stories is contemporary and no archaeological evidence has yet been found to substantiate them. This is not intended to be a statement of refutation but it is a *caveat* and also a challenge. The discovery of an early Islamic site will be as welcome as the discovery of a classical or neo-classical site.

The most striking change from the description in the *Periplus* is that the trade of the coast has now separated from the trade of the coast of Gulf of Aden. The merchants are no longer the merchants of the Yemen, but the merchants of the Persian Gulf and Oman. The trade has also reached the Comoros, the lands of the Zambezi, and the great island of Madagascar. The products of this new area of commercial exploitation were ivory, slaves and gold.

The trade in ivory was probably the most important, the

most general, and the least subject to fluctuations in political conditions. Masudi mentions also that it was seldom used in Africa because of its value as an export—a statement which is confirmed by the rarity of ivory objects found in excavations. Masudi states specifically that it was the merchants of Oman who supplied the needs of the Indian and Chinese markets. A hundred years later, Al-Biruni mentions that the prosperity of the port of Soumenat on the north coast of India was based on the African trade. Some of the earliest Islamic glazed earthenware found in East Africa, the green and yellow *sgraffiato*, is identical with sherds from the ports of Tiz and Dabul in what is now Pakistan.

The slave trade is not specifically mentioned, but the fact that it was of considerable importance is attested by the prominent part taken by the Zenj soldiers of Abu'l Abbas, the first Abbasid Khalif, in the Mosul massacre of A.D.749, and still more by the great slave revolt in southern Iraq, a hundred years later, which took fifteen years to suppress. There are also references in Chinese manuscripts to slaves from both the lands of the Zenj and Madagascar. Later in the twelfth century there is a reference in Idrisi to a ruler of Qais, the port in the Persian Gulf, which succeeded Siraf in importance, who raided the East African coast for slaves. The references in the history of Kilwa and in the travels of Ibn Battuta to the wars of the Sultans of Kilwa and Mombasa are probably operations of this nature. Finally, at the end of the fifteenth century, there was the brief rule of the African Mameluks at Gaur in Bengal.

The third principal commodity, gold, is the last to be mentioned and may not have been an article of commerce before the tenth century. Sofala is referred to by Masudi as a land of gold, and in the tenth century the gold mint of Oman began striking coins and was almost certainly using the gold of Sofala.

The issue was not of long duration and ceased when the Seljuk Turks overthrew the Buwayhid Amirs and occupied Baghdad. This meant that the gold of central Asia was once more available. The sixteenth-century Portuguese writer, Barros, mentions that the first people to export gold from Sofala were the merchants of Mogadishu. The foundation of Mogadishu is ascribed to the beginning of the tenth century—in fact to the time of Masudi—but it is possible that it had not been established by the time of his visit. By the end of the twelfth century the gold trade had passed into the hands of Kilwa. The gold was paid for with cloth and services, including the despatch of young men who would reside in Sofala, marry a reasonable number of young women and thereby produce a mixed race, which was considered a good thing. The original treaty was made with Mogadishu but later this most favoured treatment was acquired by Kilwa and with it the gold trade. The prosperity of Kilwa was in fact due to its control of the gold trade of Sofala, and its decline in the later fourteenth century, subsequent recovery, and further decline may be due to upheavals and disagreements in the hinterland from which the gold came.

It is not until we arrive at the twelfth century that archaeological data is available. The material, however, is still meagre. There is a single inscription at Kizimkazi in Zanzibar. There are also groups of *sgraffiato*, a green and yellow glazed ware, from other sites, such as Kisimani Mafia, Kilwa and Ras Makabe in Tanganyika, which can reasonably be dated to the same century. At the end of the century there is the confusing account of the coast in the geography of Idrisi. A number of towns are mentioned, including Merca, Barawa, Malindi and probably Mombasa. The picture is also filled out by the stories in the histories of Kilwa, Lamu, Pate and the 'Kitab al Zanuj', all nineteenth-century revisions but based on earlier works.

When we get to the thirteenth century we have a reasonable amount of archaeological material: inscriptions, a few coins, buildings, and the evidence of the excavations at Kilwa, Gedi, Ungwana and other sites. In the fourteenth century there is Ibn Battuta's eye-witness account of Mogadishu, Mombasa and Kilwa. All along the coast were Arab–African townships and settlements, mostly independent, ruled by Arab and Swahili families among which was one sheikhly family from whom the ruler was taken. Their relations with the African tribes were on a treaty basis, sometimes hostile, sometimes a commercial partnership. The culture of the coast was overwhelmingly Muslim and Arab. The shadowy King of the Zenj at Mombasa mentioned by Idrisi had given way to an Arab sheikh. In the extreme south, the King of the Zenj was now the Monomotapa, whose domains in the fifteenth century extended over most of Mashonaland and Manicaland.

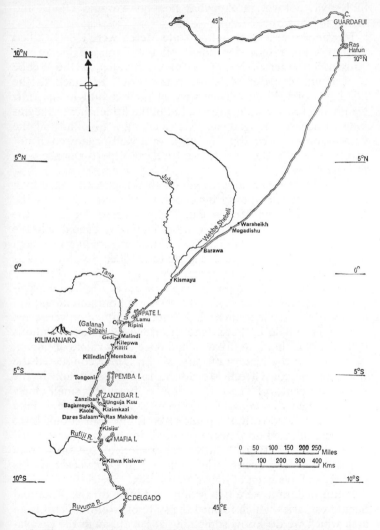

5. The East African Seaboard showing places mentioned in the text

E

The most important of these settlements were Mogadishu and Barawa in Somalia; Lamu, Pate, Malindi and Mombasa in Kenya; a town in Zanzibar possibly Unguja Ukuu, and Kilwa in Tanzania.

Mogadishu and its daughter state Merca were closely allied and to some extent dependent on the Somali tribe of the Ajuran. Together they exploited the rich valley of the Webbe Shebeli and a profitable trade route which extended to the highlands of Ethiopia. They were at their height in the thirteenth and fourteenth centuries, but in the fifteenth were beginning to decline. Mogadishu was ruled by a Sheikh, and the description given by Ibn Battuta is of a well-organized, if not luxurious, city state, able to put on a good performance with modest props.

Barawa never elected a hereditary sheikh but was ruled by a committee. Its prosperity depended to a great extent on the same conditions as Mogadishu. The suspected decline of the Benadir coast in the fifteenth century may have been due to the expansion of the Amhara Kings of Ethiopia who diverted much of the trade to the alternative route to the Red Sea, which was more easily controlled by them.

Lamu and Pate were the principal towns of the Lamu archipelago. Lamu must always have been the commercial capital in view of its excellent anchorage, but the political power seems to have been held by Pate. Pate was ruled by a line of Sultans from the Nabahani family who had once been rulers of Oman. According to the history of Pate, Sultan Omar conquered the whole of the coast from Mogadishu to Cape Delgado in the fourteenth century. The title of Jumbe, borne by small chiefs of the Tanganyika coast, is said to refer to the Palace at Pate and to be derived from the name given to the household slaves who were allotted administrative posts in the conquered territories. However, there is no corroboration of the story from the Kilwa history or any other source. If it ever occurred, it is unlikely to have been of long duration.

South of Lamu were two groups of towns on the Tana and Sabaki estuaries which formed the state of Malindi. This is an area which we do know something about through the excavations at Ungwana, near Kipini, at the mouth of the Tana (probably the Oja of the Portuguese) and at Gedi and Kilepwa near Malindi. The Sheikh of Malindi told the Portuguese that he was the rightful lord of the whole stretch of Formosa Bay, and his statement is supported to some extent by the identity of the pottery found in the early levels of these sites. This identity, however, did not continue and there is a significant difference between the local earthenware and Islamic wares of the Tana river and Malindi areas in late fifteenth- and sixteenth-century levels.

Beyond Malindi was Mombasa, the rising town of the coast, whose Sheikh is said to have been a governor appointed by the Sultan of Zanzibar and an offshoot of the royal house of Kilwa. This may not be the whole truth, there may have been an earlier sheikhly house at Mombasa related to Kilwa. It is curious that Ibn Battuta, who always succeeded in meeting the best people, never saw the Sheikh when he visited Mombasa in 1331. The aggressive policy of the Sheikh of Mombasa was the most important political fact on the coast of East Africa at the time of the arrival of the Portuguese. This enmity between Mombasa and Malindi, plus the Portuguese guns, enabled the Portuguese to establish themselves in an unfortified settlement at Malindi and to remain on relatively good terms with the Sultan of Zanzibar who, so far as Mombasa was concerned, regarded himself as an injured party.

Zanzibar, whatever she may have been in the twelfth century, was not of great importance later. The history of Pate says that she was not conquered by Sultan Omar in the fourteenth century because she was of small account. However, we know very little about the question. Some of the coins of Kilwa type which cannot be fitted into the history of Kilwa almost certainly were struck in Zanzibar, which may be a sign of some importance. Tanzania, except for Kilwa, had apparently no major towns, though there was a Sheikh at Mtangata, the present Tongoni (the predecessor of Tanga) and there was a large town at Kaole, the predecessor of Bagamoyo.

Kilwa was the nearest to a state in the European and Asiatic sense. Its domains included the settlements on the coast up to Kilwa Kivinje and possibly to the Rufiji, the island of Mafia, and in the south Mozambique and Sofala. It was probably at its height in the twelfth and thirteenth centuries and had a return of prosperity in the fifteenth, when the Great Mosque, the finest surviving mosque in East Africa, was rebuilt. It struck a copper coinage of a single denomination from the beginning of the thirteenth century, which may have been a

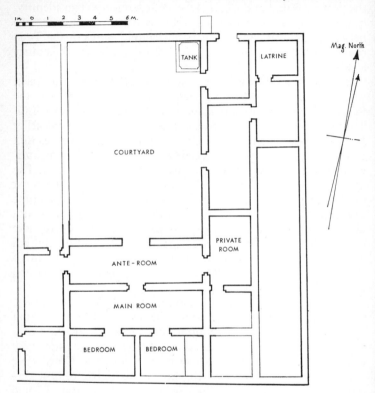

Figure VI Plan of a typical medieval coastal house
(Songo Mnara after P. S. Garlake)

matter of prestige rather than of commercial convenience. There was a Sultan who was said to be descended from a Sultan of Shiraz, whom it has been impossible to identify from Arabic sources. In the fifteenth century the throne was usurped by one of the court officials. The offices of Qadhi and Amir are said to have been granted to settlers from Malindi, and there is an old mosque, known as the Malindi mosque, which is evidence of the presence of Malindi immigrants. The ruin of Kilwa by the Portuguese and the absence of any real recovery has left it with the largest number of surviving public buildings of any town on the coast.

The Arab African towns of the coast were at their apogee when the Portuguese burst into the Indian Ocean and upset the whole pattern of trade. The main trunk routes between India and the Red Sea, and India and the Persian Gulf were interrupted and the feeder lines suffered equally. So far as East Africa was concerned, the principal interruption was in the gold trade with India, which the Portuguese attempted to monopolize. Although individual Portuguese made quite a lot out of it, the result ultimately was that there was no trade for anybody. A striking illustration of the dangers of killing a goose that lays golden eggs before you have a similar goose of your own.

There were other nuisances, such as the trading permits which the Portuguese endeavoured with varying success to impose on the Arab and Indian traders, and the frequently unjust and unauthorized exactions of the Portuguese captains. These operations, besides the capital loss caused by the destruction of Kilwa (1505), Mombasa (1505 and 1528), Zanzibar (1503 and 1509), Oja (1505), Barawa (1505) succeeded in breaking the morale and destroying the wealth of the Arab–African settlements on the coast.

The Portuguese control of the coast was exercised by the two captaincies of Sofala, later Mozambique and Kilwa, later Malindi and finally Mombasa. Both captains were responsible to the Viceroy of Goa from whom they drew their supplies and to whom they appealed in times of crisis. They paid a large sum for their appointment, which was normally for three years, during which they hoped to recoup themselves. Their duties were to maintain the loyalty of the King of Portugal's overseas subjects; to ward off the King's enemies; and to further the collection of revenue for the King by the exchange of trade goods, mostly from India, for ivory, gold, and copper.

The Captain of Malindi had the easier but generally less lucrative post. However, the raids of the Turkish privateer Mirale Bey in 1586 and 1589 shook the whole Portuguese position in his area. A strong expedition from Goa took the Turkish fleet in the harbour of Mombasa, captured the admiral, and restored the coast to obedience. It was then decided to build Fort Jesus at Mombasa as a strong point to protect the coast against Turks, Dutch and English, who were all considered dangerous enemies. Incidentally it would neutralize for ever the inveterate hostility of Mombasa which all through the sixteenth century had been the centre of resistance to the Portuguese. The Portuguese station was moved from Malindi to Mombasa in 1593 and with it moved the Sheikh of Malindi, now Sultan of Malindi and Mombasa.

The amicable relations between Sultan and Captain did not survive the departure of the first captain, Mateus Mendez de Vasconcelos, one of the ablest officials to serve in East Africa. There was the continual argument about the share of the customs which the Sultan should enjoy; an obscure, probably rather phoney claim to Pemba, which was the main source of supplies for Mombasa; and the inherent shortage of money in a country that was no Mexico or Peru.

The second Sultan was murdered by a villainous Portuguese captain, and the third and last revolted and killed all the Portuguese, including the women and children. This occurred on 15 August 1631 and perhaps marks the change from a policy of alliance, thin though it had always appeared, to a policy of subjection. The victorious Sultan left Mombasa in a Portuguese galleon and became a pirate. He had had rather a complicated education and found that he disliked his fellow-Arabs quite as much as he disliked the Portuguese.

The Portuguese reoccupied the Fort and resumed their control of the coast as far north as the Lamu archipelago; in fact, it had seldom reached much farther. But in the second half of the century a new adversary appeared in the Yaarubi Sultan of Oman, and a new centre of resistance in the town of Pate. The Portuguese town of Mombasa was sacked in 1661, and Mozambique in 1670, but the Omanis could make no impression on the two great fortresses, Fort Jesus and San Sebastião. In 1678 Pate was sacked and again reoccupied in 1687. However the sands were running out. On 13 March 1696 a large fleet arrived from Muscat, picked up reinforcements in Pate, and sailed to Mombasa. The expedition established itself at

Kilindini and commenced the siege of Fort Jesus. On 13 December 1698 Fort Jesus fell, after a siege of two years and nine months, when the Portuguese garrison had been reduced to the Captain and eight men. The details of the first twenty months of the siege have been recorded and make very good reading.

With Fort Jesus the whole Portuguese position north of Cape Delgado collapsed. Nevertheless the expulsion of the Portuguese did not mean the return of the old days of happy parochial independence and comfortable if not over-luxurious living. This was to wait another hundred years until another Sultan of Oman was to make his capital in Zanzibar.

The African background had changed during the two hundred years of Portuguese domination and to the detriment of the towns on the coast. The long war between the Galla and Somali and the Negus of Ethiopia had interrupted the trade routes between Ethiopia and the towns of Benadir. It had also promoted the southern thrust of the Galla against the Bantu tribes on the Juba and the Tana and the Arab settlements on the coast. By the middle of the seventeenth century, the northern frontier of Bantuland on the coast had been pushed back to Kilifi, 37 miles from Mombasa, and most of the Arab settlements on the mainland had been abandoned. Oja continued to be mentioned to the end of the century, but Malindi disappeared about 1667; Gedi, Kilepwa and Kilifi had gone much earlier. Post-Ming or even Transitional Ming porcelain is extremely rare on the coast of Kenya, though it is of course found on the islands of Lamu, Pate and Mombasa.

The history of the southern captaincy was somewhat different. The Arab traders continued to compete with the Portuguese longer for the gold of Zambezia, and it was not until towards the end of the sixteenth century that this competition was broken. The most important factor in the South was the existence of gold and silver mines, and the efforts of the Portuguese to find them and exploit them. In 1571 and again from 1609 to 1631, great efforts were made with this end in view, which resulted in disaster. However, large amounts of gold were obtained by traders, and Portuguese settlements were established well up the river. The Portuguese made themselves a much greater presence in the south than they ever did in the

north, though the feeble authority of the officials of Sena and
Tete over the Portuguese and mulatto barons of the Zambezi
valley could hardly be considered administration. Their treaty
relations with the Monomotapa and other chiefs were similar
to their relations with the sheikhs of the coast, although the
African chiefs were always in a stronger position. The empire
of the Monomotapa 'The Lord of the Ravaged Lands' was
probably in decline on the eve of the arrival of the Portuguese.
His southern tributaries were already independent. Although
the Portuguese with their guns had introduced a new factor of
disunion, they did to some extent preserve the fiction of a
supreme ruler by the support they gave to the various Monomotapa. The Monomotapa played a clever enough diplomatic
game, whose duplicity was largely extenuated by the double
dealing of the Portuguese.

In the Portuguese records there is ample material for the
reconstruction of the history of this part of the coast, and there
are a number of able scholars working on it—Axelson, Lobato
and Abrahams, whose work can be unreservedly recommended. There has been so far no archaeological excavation.
Dr. Abrahams has been able to record some interesting oral
traditions from a descendant of the Monomotapa. Unlike most
places on other parts of the coast, there was something of a
hereditary African monarchy in which these traditions were
preserved, and settled areas to which they could be attached.
Among the Somali there is a proud genealogical tradition, but
much of its interest is lessened by the absence of topographical
references. In the lands between, the population has changed
so frequently or has remained so disunited that apparently
nothing has survived.

By 1700 the decaying towns of Mogadishu, Merca and
Barawa had rapidly fallen into the hands of the Somali—
no longer the Arabized Ajuran but the primitive Abgal. The
Swahili Sultanate of Pate was nominally subject to the Sultan of
Oman, whilst the mainland and the ruined Arab towns were
in the hands of the Galla. Mombasa and Zanzibar were ruled
by Arab governors from Oman, Kilwa retained its Sultan but
he was very poor and in the hands of the governor of Zanzibar,
who also exercised control over the decaying towns of the
mainland opposite. Beyond was the Portuguese colonial gover-

nor at Mozambique with officers at Ibo on the Kerimba Islands, Queliman, Sena and Tete. He had some authority by treaty with the African chiefs, and perhaps rather less by respect with the Portuguese and mulatto feudal lords of the Zambezi basin. His financial and military resources were equally meagre, his interests mainly commercial. The home Government had found Brazil a far more profitable and easier land to develop.

The tribal history of the coast, behind and between the foreign towns is unknown. It may not have amounted to very much. In the north the Somalis replaced the Galla in the Benadir. Over the enormous area between Kismayu and the Zambezi there is a complete blank. The Wak-Wak of the Arab authors may be the Makua of Portuguese East Africa who are certainly the oldest tribe on the coast in their present position. The Giriama relate that there was a tribe of pygmies, the Birikimo, in the hills between Malindi and Mombasa when their ancestors arrived in the sixteenth century. There was occasional trade between the interior and the coast. The Portuguese author de Barros relates a story of a group of Africans who came down the Sabaki with gold and ivory about the middle of the fifteenth century, but this is mentioned as something extraordinary, and except in the gold trade area of the Zambezi, perhaps also by the Ruvuma, there was little contact between coast and interior.

In the sixteenth century there was the upheaval in southern Somalia which brought the Nyika and Arab–African groups like the Kilindini into Kenya in flight from the Galla. The most colourful of these were the Segeju first described by Monclaro in 1569 when they were living behind Malindi. In 1589 they combined with the Portuguese and the Arabs to destroy the cannibal horde of the Zimba as they swarmed over the walls of Malindi. Subsequently they defeated and killed in quick succession the Sheikhs of Malindi and Mombasa. However, they were not able to stand up to the Galla and in the late seventeenth century they are found at Vumba, having made a detour through the hills to the coast.

The situation in Tanzania is even more obscure but there is a large habitation site of dry stone walling, Engaruka, in the Serengetti which may go back to the Portuguese or even pre-Portuguese period. There are also the walled villages in the

Tanga area, some of which may go back to the seventeenth century.

Over most of the coast, the Africans were not unduly affected by the operations of the Portuguese. In Mombasa, there were numbers of converts, some of whom suffered martyrdom at the time of Yusuf bin Hassan. During the great siege of Fort Jesus, the local African tribes particularly the 'King' of Chonyi were glad to supply the garrison with food in exchange for cloth. Another party showed their loyalty by killing a number of Arabs and bringing their heads to the Fort. An Arab punitive expedition sent on to the mainland was forced to return with heavy losses. In the fight between the Arabs and Portuguese in Africa, the Africans did not consider themselves concerned. In the south, in the Zambezi, the situation was very different and the big-scale trade in slaves from the 'prasidios' had already started in the middle of the seventeenth century.

11 *Kilwa*

Kilwa was the most wealthy of the towns which flourished on the East African coast in the centuries preceding the arrival of the Portuguese, and the one about which we have the most historical information, which can be supplemented by evidence obtained from archaeological excavations and from an examination of surviving buildings. Mr. Kirkman in the preceding chapter has given an admirable summary of the accepted history of the coast; I shall attempt to give some account of the way of life and material culture of Kilwa, setting out first what we learn from Portuguese sources about the people and their city at the beginning of the sixteenth century, and adding what we can deduce from the archaeological evidence.

The town of Kilwa was at the northern end of the island of the same name, which was separated from the mainland by the straits which formed the harbour, somewhat over a mile wide. It seems to have extended for about three-quarters of a mile along the shore, and perhaps three or four hundred yards inland. Portuguese estimates of the population vary from 4,000 to 12,000 persons. They consisted of light-skinned 'Moors' (probably Arabs), who do not seem to have been numerous, black 'Moors' (no doubt the equivalent of the present-day Swahili), to which group the ruling families appear to have belonged, and Africans. These last were evidently mostly slaves and chiefly employed in work on the plantations. The Portuguese were much impressed with the richness of the clothing of the more prosperous people: both men and women wore fine garments of silk and cotton, and there was much jewellery of gold and silver—both arm and leg ornaments, and ear-rings. Slaves, however, wore a loin-cloth only.

For food, there were cattle, sheep, goats, chickens and of course, fish. The chief grain crop was sorghum or millet. There were many coconut palms and plenty of vegetables and fruit—chiefly oranges and lemons. The betel was cultivated for chewing to extract the narcotic juice, and cotton of very high quality was grown. Very many spindle whorls have been found in the excavations, and attest that the cotton was spun and no doubt woven.

Their boats ran up to fifty tons, and were evidently of the *mtepe* type, being built of planks sewn together with coir cords. For weapons they relied chiefly on bows and arrows; they used few swords and no muskets, but disposed of a number of catapults.

The exports of Kilwa included gold, silver and pearls, together with glass, perfume, cotton goods and gum copal; all except the last two were in fact re-exports. Of these, gold, derived from the hinterland of Kilwa's dependency Sofala 900 miles to the south, was certainly much the most significant We know from other sources that ivory was also an important item of trade, and rice, probably cultivated on the mainland, was exported too. The trade in slaves would seem to have been almost non-existent at this period.

Such, then, is the evidence from the books on which we base our picture of Kilwa in the first years of the sixteenth century. For earlier times, the only eye-witness account we have is that of Ibn Battuta, who visited the place in 1331. He writes: 'The city of Kilwa is one of the finest and most substantially built towns; all the buildings are of wood and the houses are roofed with *dis* reeds.'[1] The last part of this statement can hardly be correct, as we shall see; Ibn Battuta's memory must be at fault, as it not infrequently was, which is hardly surprising as his account was dictated many years after the event. But we can deduce that most of the buildings were houses of mud and wattle. The majority of the inhabitants were Zinj, jet black in colour, who tattooed their faces. The sultan, who was noted for his piety and generosity, made frequent expeditions against the heathen Zinj people of the mainland, devoting the fifth of the booty to charity, as required by the Koran.

Let us now see what archaeology has to add to the picture. On the historical aspects, my conclusions are still tentative, for

[1] The reading and translation of this passage put forward by G. S. P. Freeman-Grenville in the *Uganda Journal*, vol. 19, p. 5, in his *Medieval History of Tanganyika*, p. 106 and in *East African Coast, Select Documents*, p. 31, is not acceptable.

our excavations are not yet completed. It seems probable, however, that Ali ibn al-Hasan (otherwise al-Husein) who is put forward in the Kilwa Chronicle as the 'founder' of Kilwa, really existed as an historical personage, and I am inclined to think that he was the first person to have struck coins at Kilwa. At the same time I believe that the accepted date of the arrival of this King and the immigrants from 'Shiraz' (probably to be interpreted as from the Persian Gulf) is too early by about two centuries, and that the true date of the settlement of this group at Kilwa is most likely to be in the second half of the twelfth century. At the same time Kilwa would have had a history extending back several centuries before the 'Shirazis' arrived; when the first people settled, the site of the town was, it seems, little more than a sand-spit a foot or two above the highest tides, and the present height of the land surface in the area (about fifteen feet) is entirely due to the accumulation of rubbish and of successive building periods. The original settlement probably dates from the ninth century A.D.

We cannot say much yet about the way of life of the earliest settlers, since very little of these inaccessible depths have been excavated. At the lowest levels we have as yet found no structures and little imported material; the characteristic local pottery is a fine graphite-burnished ware. Above this is a long period, represented by six to eight feet of deposit, when Kilwa was chiefly a town of houses built with red soil, presumably over a wattle framework. This red soil is sandy, with a clay binding element; it is acknowledged to be the best plastering material at the present day, but as it has to be brought from some distance it is now only used for special work, such as ceilings. At the same time there was a certain amount of building in stone during this period thought to precede the 'Shirazi' immigration; but we have not yet found evidence of the use of lime mortar. No coins have been found in these early levels; one would expect any that await discovery to have been imported from other lands bordering the Indian Ocean.

The period of the first 'Shirazi' sultans is marked by a noticeable increase in building in stone, though it is probable that the great majority of houses were of the same type as in the previous period. The quality of construction attained a standard never subsequently achieved, the masonry being of roughly squared coral blocks set more or less in courses and bedded in lime mortar, with fine-cut stone quoins. To this period (possibly late twelfth to mid-thirteenth century) are ascribed the earliest stages of the Great Mosque.

The succeeding period—put tentatively at from around 1250 to 1350—represents the apogee of the civilization of Kilwa. Only here in equatorial Africa do we find evidence of life being lived on the grand scale, and an architecture which goes beyond the merely practical. Probably early in this period were built the two enormous structures outside the town proper (about a mile east of its centre), with the excavation of which we have been largely occupied during the last three years.

They are built on cliffs overlooking the sea, and are known locally as Husuni Kubwa and Husuni Ndogo. As their names imply (husuni—a fortress in Swahili) they look at first sight as if they have a defensive purpose, but in fact it is very unlikely that they were built with military ends in view.

Like all the stone buildings of the coast, they are built of coral rag, obtained from the reefs, set in lime mortar, which, except where it has decayed through the action of roots and other causes, is exceedingly hard. It is evident that an architect was employed and that the masons worked from plans, for the buildings are set out with great accuracy, and show a balanced and, where feasible, regular layout. From the nature of the plans it seems very probable that the architect learnt his trade in the Arab homelands, probably Iraq.

The smaller of the two buildings consists of a massive rectangular enclosure wall with solid towers at the corners and at intervals along the side. The importance of the building is that it is the only structure of this type found up till now in tropical Africa; in style it resembles the outer walls of early mosques in Iraq and elsewhere and also caravanserais[1] in Persia. As to date, it appears to be contemporary with Husuni Kubwa, and hence of the thirteenth century.

Husuni Kubwa is much the largest pre-European building yet found on the East African coast; it was almost certainly built as a palace for one of the Kilwa sultans. It consists essentially of a number of courtyards, mostly at a lower level than the rest of the building, surrounded by long narrow

[1] An inn with a great inner court.

rooms, often ranged in rows, up to five in number, one in front
of the other. The core of the complex, the whole of which
covers about two acres, is disposed in a regular plan about a
north–south axis, the shape of the whole being governed by the
configuration of the spur of land on which it was built—a
situation which seems to have been chosen for the fine view
over the harbour and the cool breezes which the site affords.
The main entrance is by way of a wide flight of steps leading
up from the shore; it is probable that the sultan moved about
by boat for choice, the coolest and quickest way of getting to
and from the town.

The rooms were some ten feet high, airy and no doubt cool,
but rather dark. Their floors were of plaster, in many cases
provided with drains in the centre, leading into a conical stone
soak-away. The walls were white plastered; in certain of the
rooms rows of holes indicate that they were ornamented with
wall hangings—or carved wooden friezes. Most of the roofs
were flat, and constructed of cut coral blocks laid on cut
timbers, with a very thick layer of stone and lime concrete
above. The weight of these roofs restricted the width of the
rooms, which were consequently usually long and somewhat
narrow (about nine feet). Parts of the building, including
some of the chief reception-rooms, were of two stories, the
upper being roofed with domes and vaults of various designs.
For these vaults cut stone voussoirs were employed—a style
which we can also see in the Great Mosque in the town. Cut
coral stone of fine quality was used also for the jambs of doors,
and for decorative stonework and inscriptions built into the
walls. The inscriptions are in Arabic—though we know that
Swahili was spoken on the coast at this time we have no direct
evidence that it was being written; Swahili nicknames occur,
however, in the Kilwa Chronicle. On the other hand the Portuguese write of the 'Moors' speaking Arabic, and they may well
have been bilingual. The texts are in the cursive script, but in
various styles, two of them highly ornamented and sophisticated. One particularly well-cut long inscription includes all
the pointing, and is in faultless Arabic; another gives us the
name of al-Hasan bin Sulaiman, probably a sultan of that
name who lived in the thirteenth century.

The most luxurious of the appointments of the palace is the

bathing pool, an octagonal structure which would have held some 20,000 gallons. This must, it seems, have been filled by hand with water obtained from wells (of which there are two, one of very great size), which presupposes a large force of servants, or more probably, slaves.

This palace, then, reflects a spacious way of life and a considerable degree of skill and sophistication in its architecture. We should not, of course, expect anything so advanced in the dwellings of lesser persons, many of whom no doubt lived in houses of mud and timber, but a comparable standard was attained in the mosque. Parts of the Great Mosque probably date back to the late twelfth or early thirteenth century. Here the style and technique is in certain respects similar to those described, but columns, which are not found in the palace, are employed, and greater use is made of arches. Most of this building, however, and all the other 'medieval' mosques, are of the fifteenth century, by which time we can detect some deterioration in standards. Pillars are no longer cut from a single block of stone, but built up with mortar, and domes and vaults are of poured lime concrete. Nevertheless, the workmanship is exceedingly good, for two of these buildings remain substantially intact after 500 years, without apparently having undergone any significant repairs during this period.

In domestic architecture, we find in the fourteenth and fifteenth centuries the same scheme of rows of rooms set one in front of the other as we have described above, together with sunken courtyards, the latter within the building rather than in front of the entrance as at Gedi. One large house of this period began with a single story, a second being added later. Such later building is found to be of a quality inferior to the earlier. Slots in the masonry attest the use of heavy wooden doors; we know that some at least of these were carved, probably somewhat after the style of those made until modern times on the coast. Many latrines, well fitted out in cut stone, with an ablution place adjoining, are provided. Cooking seems to have been carried out over round jar-like stoves set in the floor, and also over movable three-horned pots (the cooking vessel resting on the horns over a charcoal fire lit within the pot) such as were used until recently on sailing vessels. Wells were built of stone, and water was stored in cisterns within the houses.

In the fifteenth century began a new mode of decoration—that of setting bowls of colourful imported Chinese celadon porcelain and Islamic pottery in the undersides of domes and vaults, and probably also in walls. To a large extent this seems to have replaced ornament in cut stone. Farther north—from the region of Dar es Salaam up into the Somali Republic—we

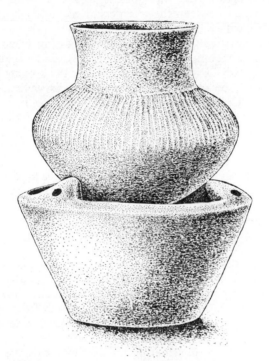

Figure VII Cooking pot of 'wealed ware' and portable stove, from Kilwa

Fifteenth century. Total height 34 cm. (13½ inches)

find bowls set into the face of the pillars which are the outstanding features of the 'medieval' tombs of that region. At Kilwa almost all of the graves of the period seem to have been marked by simple sandstone slabs, or by a plain kerb with a tombstone within. There are, however, two grave enclosures

with arched doorways after the style of the mosque architecture
which are thought to contain the graves of sultans.

Of the movables of the people of Kilwa, much the commonest material which has survived is pottery; wood and other
organic materials have of course vanished. The glazed ware
was all imported; at the beginning of the sixteenth century
about two-thirds of this was Chinese porcelain, being roughly
equally divided between the green celadons and the blue-and-
white Ming, with a little stoneware. The latter was the material
of storage jars; we find too, a few large jars in celadon, but
most of the porcelains are bowls and dishes, evidently used for
table-ware, and, as already remarked, for ornament. It must
not, however, be imagined that these vessels were imported
direct from China; we know that the Chinese never sailed
farther south in their ships than northern Kenya, and this was
an exceptional voyage. The Chinese goods were probably trans-
shipped either in India or in the Persian Gulf, or both.

The Islamic wares were no doubt imported direct from the
Gulf. The commonest early type is the *sgraffiato*, a ware decorated with a pattern incised through the slip, and with a
variegated yellow-brown-green glaze; this is on most of the
coast is typical of the thirteenth century and earlier and not
normally associated with any Chinese porcelain. By the beginning of the sixteenth century, however, Islamic pottery only
forms about a third of the imported ware, and is mostly of the
plain monochrome blue-and-green glazed type. Chinese wares
were evidently preferred for the table, and such good quality
Persian pottery as was imported was used rather for ornament-
ing roofs. Unglazed porous water-jars, decorated in relief, were
also imported in small quantities.

It is remarkable, considering the standard of development
attained, that nowhere on the East African coast was any
glazed pottery produced; nor do the people seem to have ever
made use of the potter's wheel. There is some uniformity in the
unglazed wares of the coast in the earlier period, but in general
they varied from region to region, and there does not seem to
have been a great deal of coastwise trade in pottery. At Kilwa
the local pottery is somewhat more sophisticated than farther
north, but nevertheless on the whole simple. Table-ware is
decorated with simple designs in red paint, or coated with red

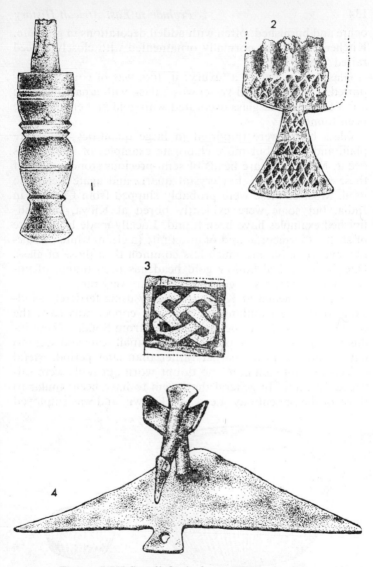

Figure VIII Small finds from Tanzania sites

1 *Ivory finial from Kilwa* Probably fifteenth century Length 7·5 cm. **2** *Top of a comb of Ivory from Tongoni* Probably fifteenth century Length 2·8 cm. **3** *Carved ivory inlay from Tongoni* Probably fifteenth century Length 2·8 cm. **4** *Bronze object, perhaps a lid, from Kilwa* Fourteenth century, possibly of Indian origin Length 11·8 cm.

ochre and burnished, often with added decorations in graphite.
Kitchen vessels are normally ornamented with closely spaced
raised 'weals' of clay.

Glass was evidently a luxury; it, too, was of course all imported. The most usual vessel was a flask with a narrow neck;
a few fragments of glass decorated with gold and enamel have
been found.

Glass beads were imported in large quantities; most are
plain and small, but more elaborate examples of inlaid glass
occur. Much rarer are beads of semi-precious stones; most of
these were carnelian, but crystal quartz and agate were also
used. Most of these were probably shipped from Cambay in
India, but some were evidently bored at Kilwa, for half-
finished examples have been found. Locally made beads were
of shell, of terracotta, and of aragonite (a clean, white marble-
like material), but are much less common than those of glass.
One finely worked hollow gold bead has been found, of uncertain date. Objects of gold and ivory are very rare.

Iron was smelted at Kilwa (probably using ferricrete sandstone from the mainland as ore) and copper was cast, the
copper itself probably being imported from Sofala. These industries, however, were probably on a small scale and seem to
have flourished in the earlier rather than later period. Metal
objects are not common—no doubt worn-out tools were sal-
vaged for scrap. In general they seem to have been similar to
those of the present day. Lead was known, and was employed

Figure IX Weights, of bronze over lead, Kilwa

Fifteenth century. The larger one weighs 15¼ oz.

for weights covered with copper and ornamented with incised decoration.

Coins, of copper, and all of one denomination, were minted in large quantities by certain (but not all) of the sultans from the late twelfth century onwards, but few were struck after the middle of the fourteenth century.[1] These bear the names of the rulers and afford a valuable means of checking the accuracy of the Kilwa Chronicle. The coinage does not seem to have circulated to the mainland, and is not found north of Zanzibar (where coins were also minted); Mogadishu had its own currency. Foreign Muslim coins are otherwise absent, in contrast to Kisimani Mafia, where thirteenth-century coins from Egypt, Persia and India have been found. Coins of silver are lacking; probably the copper currency served as small change only. Large transactions, and all trade with the interior would have been carried on by barter or for coastal commerce with gold; a

Figure X Copper coin of Sulaiman ibn al-Hasan,
Sultan of Kilwa c. A.D. 1294–1306

Rhyming obverse and reverse reads: Obv. *Sulaiman bin/al-Hasan* Sulaiman son of al-Hasan; Rev: *Yathiqu bi Maul/al-Minan*, He Trusts in the Master of Bounties (God). With the addition of Sa'ida, 'may he be happy' on the obverse and '*azza*, 'he is glorious', on the reverse

gold coin has recently come to light in Mafia, and has been identified as probably an imitation of a gold Dinar of the Fatimid ruler al-Aziz, A.D. 975–996, struck for circulation in Palestine at the time of the Crusades.[2]

Though the prosperity of Kilwa depended entirely on the export of materials obtained from the interior (and hence when

[1] This is my personal (and tentative) view; I think that the two commonest groups of coins (those of al-Hasan bin Sulaiman and most of those of Ali bin al-Hasan) have been wrongly attributed to sultans of these names who ruled in the fifteenth century.

[2] This coin is in the possession of Mr. M. Fainsilber to whom I am grateful for making this important find available to me; for the opinion on its identity I am indebted to the late Dr. J. Walker.

the Portuguese interfered with her trade, her decline to a position of small significance was rapid) the impact of her civilization on the hinterland is hardly detectable. Inland from Sofala there was considerable penetration, and a certain amount of foreign goods reached the interior and have been found at Zimbabwe and elsewhere. On the coast, apart from this trade, and a route south-westwards from Kilwa via Lake Nyasa, it seems that no one went any distance from the seaboard. It was rather the tribesmen who came to the Islamic settlements which sprinkled the coast, taking away with them cloth and beads, but little else.

PART FOUR

Oral Traditions, History and the Remembered Past of East Africa

Oral traditions provide the essential basis for much of African history. Until very recently, due largely to ignorance of local languages amongst the expatriate scholars, these traditions have been neglected as a source of history except by the social anthropologists. In many ways they are the most accessible of all the sources of African history for the African student and provide a wide scope for the local historian to make a contribution to our knowledge. The traditions are being looked at from many different viewpoints the cumulative effect of which is to highlight the items of value in the traditions and to indicate the various drawbacks of relying on them too completely.

The collection of the traditions requires a specialist or at least a disciplined approach whilst their interpretation, as the following essays indicate, depends on the interpreter having a sound knowledge of the society of which the traditions form an integral part. The traditions, though of value to the historian, have significance also to the linguist, the anthropologist, the archaeologist and the student of agricultural origins. Besides the traditions mainly relating to the courts of rulers, the histories of clans, and the customs and migrations of peoples, there are also the folk tales, the songs and the place-names which form the local colour of any area. These are the most unexplored sources of our past and ones which provide a close link with later history and literature.

The period of traditional history is the essential link between prehistory and history in the more general sense of the written word. Being a borderland it must be spanned by both disciplines and form a bridge rather than the hiatus it has formerly been.

In Africa we are more fortunate than past compilers of oral traditions, like Alfred the Great in England working through the West Saxon chronicles or the fifth and sixth century B.C.

Israel scribes rendering the Bible into a written form. The use of tape-recorders and the interdisciplinary approach of social anthropologists, topographers, etymologists, students of traditional religion and historians is revealing information that was hitherto unsuspected. Much of recent African history is a kaleidoscope of internal movement which responds well to a detailed, followed by a comparative, study of tribal traditions.

Uganda has some of the most detailed and reliable traditions in Africa, particularly in the west where some twenty generations of hereditary rulers can be traced. Each of the Kingdoms has its own traditions, some of which are comparable one with another and all are prefaced by myths about former rulers, tribal origins and the first inhabitants. The myths and legends reveal a common cosmology and help in suggesting elements in the early history. As with histories elsewhere in the world there is a tendency for each set of legends to suggest that the other Kingdoms are of more recent origin and not in the same direct relationship with the founder dynasty, in this case the Abacwezi. Besides the western traditions there are detailed accounts of the Lwoo clans of the north which are of comparable date and deal with Nilotic folk movements which were taking place at the time that the Kingdoms of the south had commenced a more stable existence.

From the traditions we glimpse a past social life and hear of the arrival of the first 'tea' cups to *Kabaka* Kyabaggu of Buganda in the eighteenth century or of the arrival of the Arabs in Kooki in southern Uganda in the 1830s. The linguists, by studying the names of the people mentioned, find evidence of Nilotic leaders amongst Bantu-speaking peoples and from place-names a suspicion lingers of the Northern Madi and Moru peoples once being more widespread to the south than they are at present. In Kenya and Tanzania, except for the people of Buhaya who have similar traditions to the Banyankore, the oral history is not as detailed and does not stretch so far back in time. Nevertheless it provides evidence of where the principal peoples came from and when, and gives clues about peoples who have disappeared as tribal units like the Sirikwa with their stone-lined hollows in the Eldoret area, or of the forest-dwelling Agumba of Central Kenya after whom the first post Stone Age archaeological cultures were named.

These traditions are of immense value in realizing the way our own African society has evolved. To study them we have to work backwards from the present, a method which is rather more straightforward to understand than the reconstruction of history using abstract millennia of past Stone Ages which seem to impinge so little on the present African scene. But all this history must be keyed into the work of the archaeologists. Archaeologists are primarily concerned with delineating cultures made up from characteristic assemblages of material objects like pots, iron tools and stone implements or of the remains of structures, earthworks and settlement sites. Oral traditions by their very nature suffer from conflationary tendencies but nevertheless the circumstantial evidence of where rulers lived, the size of their realms, the corollary of which can often be the archaeological culture, and the length of occupation of particular sites are aspects that can be checked by archaeological means. A famous example from outside East Africa of how excavations can show the validity of oral history is Schliemann's discovery of the succession of cities of Troy in Asia Minor as indicated in Homer. In Uganda the archaeological discovery that a royal capital site of Ankole at Bweyorere was occupied twice, as suggested by the traditions, similarly confirms that the traditions have some value for the archaeologist. Though in historical terms the accuracy of the dating is suspect, the relative order of antiquity arrived at by studying 'king lists' is closer than could be obtained by radiocarbon determinations or from the study of typological sequences in the absence of datable objects of the kind that are found on coastal sites.

If the traditions are able to indicate the sites for the archaeologists to excavate, the archaeologists can fill in the details of the material way of life by providing information on house types, agricultural practices, trade, crafts and industry, that the traditions ignore in their accounts of kings and princes, battles and raids, auguries and embassies.

12 *Oral Traditions and the Historian*

I. THE ROLE OF HISTORY IN SOCIETY

The maintenance and continuity of a society or institution normally necessitates the perpetuation of an historical tradition which may be written or oral. And to understand the society or institution, one has to understand its historical tradition. What, for instance, is a family without its genealogy? What is Christianity divorced from the Bible, liturgy and catechism? What is a state shorn of her constitution, treaties, laws and history? And who can hope to understand the history of an industry without taking into consideration the contracts, franchises and articles of incorporation?

And yet how often has this obvious point been ignored by many scholars who study African societies. While maintaining passionately that African societies have no history which pre-dates the colonial era, these same scholars have, on the other hand, written enormous works on such subjects as 'African religions', 'African Political Institutions', 'African Customary Law' and 'African Art'. In these works, they have amassed mountains of empirical data, constructed wonderful theoretical models, and invented tongue-twisting concepts such as 'antagonistic acculturation', 'pyramidal and consummatory' types of authority, 'consociational' systems of government, etc. Many of them have ignored the fact that contemporary institutions are themselves historical products, and they can be understood neither singly nor comparatively without attention being paid to their historical dimension. All social institutions in Africa—the family, the clan, religious cults, kingship, etc.—have traditions (living and significant traditions) which embody the ideals and values of a culture. These ideals and values, to be meaningful, must be analysed in historical depth.

The task of studying and analysing the relationships between the various social institutions in a society is usually left to the social anthropologist. But the historian is also interested in these relationships in as far as they shed some light on the dim past. This is particularly so as the functions of institutions do change over a period of time. New functions are added to social institutions and some of the old functions are dropped. Such social changes are normally embodied in the traditions of a particular society, and the historian, however orthodox he may be, cannot afford to ignore such evidence.

Furthermore, social facts pertaining to change are not self-explanatory. A social anthropologist may produce all the relevant facts on a particular aspect of social change; but history will still be essential, especially when we have conflicting social interpretations. For instance, Mr. D. W. Robertson, in his *The Historical Considerations Contributing to the Soga System of Land Tenure*, 1940, applies the conquest theory to the Soga States. On the other hand, Professor Lloyd A. Fallers, who collected his data between 1950 and 1952, maintains in his *Bantu Bureaucracy* (1956) that is is 'difficult, on the basis of present knowledge, to determine with any certainty the truth or untruth of the conquest interpretation of the Soga States'.[1] Or again, take the case of the Lango of Uganda. According to Tarantino, Driberg and many other writers, they are a Nilo–Hamitic people—part of the Karamojong stock— who by the middle of the nineteenth century had acquired a Luo tongue. Recently, Father Crazzolara, in a very controversial paper, has asserted that: 'The Lango Omiru are not Lango at all, not any more than the Acholi are, but both are Lwoo peoples, and to about the same degrees.'[2] In both of these cases, history must be the arbiter. Clan histories of the Basoga and the Lango must be carefully recorded, analysed and interpreted before we can hope to solve these important historical questions. At present we have no evidence for preferring one interpretation to the other.

It is therefore clear that if the historian's subject matter is human society or human culture treated chronologically, as I believe it must be, then no history of pre-colonial Africa which ignores the living oral traditions of the various indigenous

[1] Fallers, L. A., *Bantu Bureaucracy* (1956), p. 35.
[2] Crazzolara, J. P., Notes on the Lango-Omiru; *Anthropos*, vol. 55 (1960), p. 202.

societies can be complete. Nor can we hope to understand the social institutions of these peoples except in historical depth.

II. THE NATURE OF HISTORICAL EVIDENCE

When I decided in 1958 to study the pre-colonial history of East Africa, many of my friends and mentors ridiculed the decision on the ground that one cannot study what is non-existent. 'Where are the documents?' they asked. 'Without documents there is no history,' they reminded me again and again. But I persisted. Their arguments failed to convince me for two reasons: (a) I was unable to accept the implied thesis that the history of East Africa should be equated with the Colonial period of a mere seventy years. (b) Granted that we have to depend to a considerable degree on oral evidence for certain periods of East African History, I did not find this fact perturbing at all, for the problem of oral evidence is not peculiar to Africa.

As historical evidence, neither oral tradition nor the written word can be an accurate and dispassionate record of the past. As Gordon Childe has stated:[1] 'No chronicler nor historian can attempt to record all events; from the superfluity of happenings he must select what he regards as memorable. His selection is determined to a very small extent by his personal idiosyncrasies, but on the whole by tradition and social interests. Indeed, save for personal memoirs and diaries, the standard of the memorable is a social one, dictated by interests shared by the whole community, or more precisely by the ruling class in each community.'

European accounts of nineteenth-century history of East Africa, for instance, show the extent to which our standard of what is memorable in history can be determined by social and political factors. Many of these accounts are not only highly coloured and biased, but often they are inaccurate. The problem with much of these written sources is that most of the authors started with certain preconceived ideas about Africans which were then prevalent and which tended to mar their

[1] Childe, V. Gordon, *History* (1947), p. 22.

otherwise excellent records. To take two outstanding examples
—Speke and Burton. In the introduction to his *Journal of the
Discovery of the Source of the Nile*,[1] Speke unashamedly records
his prejudices:

I profess accurately to describe naked Africa—Africa in those places
where it has not received the slightest impulse, whether for good or
for evil, from European civilization. If the picture be a dark one, we
should when contemplating these sons of Noah, try to carry our
minds back to the time when our poor elder brother Ham was
cursed by his father, and condemned to be the slave of both Shem
and Japheth; for as they were then, so they appear to be now—a
strikingly existing proof of the Holy Scriptures. But one thing must
be remembered: Whilst the people of Europe and Asia were blessed
by Communion with God through the medium of His Prophets, and
obtained divine laws to regulate their ways and keep them in mind
of Him who made them, the Africans were excluded from this dis-
pensation, and consequently have no idea of an overruling Provi-
dence or a future State; they therefore trust to luck and to charms,
and think only of self-preservation in this world.

'The Africans', Speke continues, are 'too avaricious', 'too
destitute of fellow-feeling', and have a 'proficiency for telling
lies'. 'They are altogether a cursed lot.'[2] Viewed in these terms
is it any wonder that East Africa appeared dark and doomed!
The tendency was therefore to regard whatever contributed to
this dark picture painted by the explorers, missionaries and
consular officials as memorable, and to ignore whatever con-
tradicted it.

Speke's companion, Richard Burton, had even stronger prejudices. In his *Lake Regions of Central Africa*, he writes: 'He
(the African) seems to belong to one of those races which,
never rising to man's estate, fall like worn-out links from the
great chain of animated nature.' When on 7 November 1857
Burton met the Arab slave-traders at Kazeh, he recorded,
'Striking indeed was the contrast between the open-handed

[1] Speke, J. H., *Journal* (London, 1864), p. XIII.

[2] Julius Caesar had written in the same vein about the Britons when he
landed in England in 54 B.C., where he said he found only a collection of
naked savages, who lived like beasts in caves and holes. We now know
that there was a higher stage of culture in Britain before his time than
Caesar inferred.

hospitality and hearty goodwill of this truly noble race, and the niggardness of the savage and selfish African—it was heart of flesh after heart of stone.'[1]

And yet it was this 'truly noble race' that has, through their traffic in human beings, demoralized the African and produced the state of turmoil and insecurity that Burton described so graphically.

Intellectually, according to Burton, 'the East African is sterile and incult, apparently unprogressive and unfit for change. . . . Devotedly fond of music, his love of tune has invented nothing but whistling and the whistle: his instruments are all borrowed from the coast people. . . .'[2]

It should be clear from the passages I have cited that written evidence *per se* is no more reliable than oral evidence, especially when it emanates from such biased observers. Alan Moorehead in his readable book *The White Nile* (1960) has remarked that 'although Burton and Speke passed huge slave caravans, some of them 1,000 strong, and saw the tragic aftermath of their progress—the sick men, women and children dying beside the track—both of them made the point that the hardships of the journey were not quite as bad as they were made out to be.'[3] 'Justice required', Burton wrote, 'the confession that slave-driving rarely meets the eye in East Africa. Some merchants chain or cord together their gangs for safer transport through regions where desertion is at a premium. Usually, however, they trust rather to soft words and kind treatment; the fat lazy slave is often seen stretched at ease in the shade, whilest the master toils in the sun and wind. The "property" is well fed and little worked. . . . The relationship is rather that of patron and client than of Lord and bondsman; the slave is addressed as Ndugu yango, "my brother", and he is seldom provoked by hard words or stripes.'[4]

And yet Livingstone's experiences during his last journey were quite the opposite. 'The sights I have seen on this journey', he wrote, 'make my blood turn cold, and I am not senti-

[1] Burton, *Lake Regions* (London, 1860), p. 323.
[2] Burton, ibid., vol. II, pp. 337–8.
[3] Moorehead, *The White Nile* (London, 1960), p. 32.
[4] Burton, *Lake Regions*, vol. II, p. 367.

mental.'[1] It was, of course, the inhuman traffic that had made him sick at heart. When later he witnessed the murder of about 300 to 400 souls by the Arabs at Nyangwe, he had 'the impression of being in Hell'.

The problem of conflicting accounts of presumably similar historical events is thus no special feature of oral evidence, as some historians and anthropologists have contended. It applies to all types of historical evidence; and to exclude oral evidence from consideration on the ground that one has to deal with several conflicting versions of an historical event is merely to express a prejudice.

Secondly, for that period in a people's history when written evidence is either lacking or meagre, oral evidence, corroborated by other independent evidence, has been utilized fruitfully in most countries of the world; and there is therefore no reason why Africa should be treated differently. The great epic poems of Homer, the Song of Deborah, the Creation story and the legends of Noah and the Tower of Babel—all these poems, myths and legends are considered by most people to be of historical significance. In Uganda, for instance, the Acholi 'Bwola Songs', the Alur creation myth, and the Kintu legend are of great interest to a historian. But we must distinguish between those traditions which relate to the origins of societies and those that deal with migrations, settlements, internal relations and internal developments of peoples. The former in any society are usually expressed in myths and legends that are difficult to interpret, while the latter are normally straightforward narratives, with a sprinkling of myth and legends. It is with the second category of traditions that a historian is chiefly concerned.

As an example of the second category of traditions, let us take the case of the early Anglo-Saxon period in English History. What are the sources? Strictly speaking there are only four important sources:

(a) Gildas' *Destruction of Britain*, written by a British priest more than a hundred years after the Romans left Britain.

(b) Bede's *Ecclesiastical History*, compiled in the early eighth century.

[1] Livingstone, D., *His Life and Letters* (1957) by George Seaver, p. 554.

(c) Nennius' *History of the Britons*, written in the ninth century. This is a thoroughly unreliable book which glorifies the Britons and makes them win every battle in a war they obviously lost.

(d) The *Anglo-Saxon Chronicle*, the early part of which was probably written in the reign of Alfred the Great.

This is all of the historical evidence we have for this period —all of them compilations of oral traditions. The English historians, while regarding characters like Hengist, Horsa, Arthur and Vortigern as legendary, have nevertheless maintained that they are based on fact. What the English historians have done, say, with the *Anglo-Saxon Chronicle*, is what African historians are trying to do with oral evidence. The story as given in the *Anglo-Saxon Chronicle* is not well authenticated history as we understand it. It is a series of annals attached to dates in the fifth and sixth centuries which offer an outline of the traditional story of the settlement of Kent, Sussex, Wessex, East Anglia and Northumbria. It was composed, as we have seen, in the ninth century, from the ancestral memories of the invaders. Great English historians such as Oman, J. R. Green, Williamson, Trevelyan, Myres and Stenton have worked on this chronicle, checking and filling out, wherever possible, with the aid of the discoveries of the archaeologist and by the evidence of place names.

I have dwelt on the Anglo-Saxon history at length because there is a tendency among certain scholars to feel that what the traditional historian is doing in Africa today is something new and different. Such scholars have even refused to apply the honourable name 'history' to the study of the past of Africa, and have coined a new term for it—'ethno-history'. The fact is, as Professor Vansina has stated, that 'the study of the past of African cultures is history, uses the methods of this science and comes to conclusions which are of the same nature as historical conclusions reached in any part of the world'.[1]

In East Africa, we have large numbers of oral traditions. On the coast there are the Swahili 'histories', written in Arabic script, of towns such as Pate, Lamu, Mombasa, Kilwa, etc. These, together with archaeological findings, have already been

[1] Vansina, J., 'Recording the Oral History of the Bakuba', *Journal of African History*, vol. I, No. 1 (1960), p. 53.

used by such historians as Dr. Freeman-Grenville to reconstruct the past of East Africa.[1] Inland, there are large collections of oral traditions, both in English and French, as well as
in African languages. Several more are being compiled. Moreover, unlike the dead traditions of the Angles and Saxons, the
traditions of East African peoples are living, and several
anthropological works dealing with different facets of African
societies have recently been published. We shall soon, therefore, be in a position to write a history of East Africa which will
deal not simply with the invaders and their activities in Africa,
but with the Africans and their reactions to external stimuli.
Already an important start has been made in this direction, for
Volume I of the *Oxford History of East Africa* deals entirely
with the pre-colonial period.

III. AFRICAN HISTORIOGRAPHY

Since African historiography is part of general historiography, I shall only make a few remarks on the techniques that
African historians have evolved for handling their material,
From my experience, the problem facing the traditional historian is not that of lack of evidence, but its complexity. One is
often confronted with a wealth of conflicting stories and
traditions, sociological data, linguistic evidence, place names,
and in some cases, the discoveries of the archaeologists. With
such a bewildering variety of historical evidence, it may be
wondered whether a new methodology and training is not
desirable for the African historian. It has even been asked
where these 'super-men', who would feel at home in several
disciplines, are to come from in this age of specialization. The
important point to note here, however, is that since African
history is part of world history, we have to employ the same
historical methods in Africa which the historians have evolved
over a number of centuries. This may be exacting, but we
cannot afford to be satisfied with anything less.

In this connexion we must make a distinction between the
collection of oral traditions and their interpretation. The
administrators, the missionaries and the anthropologists who

[1] Freeman-Grenville, G. P., *The Medieval History of the Tanganyika
Coast* (Oxford, 1962).

F

pioneered this field of research tended to merge these two important processes. With a few notable exceptions such as Maurice Delafosse, the colonial administrators were limited by their lack of historical training and their sense of mission. They did not leave behind, for the historian's scrutiny, the vernacular texts, the lists of their informants, the circumstances under which the material was collected, and the manner of transmitting oral evidence in the particular societies they studied. Consequently, they presented us with accounts which are difficult to interpret. Oral traditions need to be transformed into written texts before the historian's art can be applied.

More recently, the social anthropologists have come to appreciate more fully the value of oral traditions in the study of African culture. But they too have lacked the necessary historical training; and, on the whole, they have tended to concentrate on those aspects of oral traditions which relate to their theoretical models, especially myths, legends and genealogies. In most cases they have not answered historical questions; because of the intensive and small-scale nature of many of their investigations, they have tended to ignore the historically more significant traditions such as those concerning trade-routes and external relations. Moreover, some of the historically important groups, for instance, the Palwo in Bunyoro, have been completely ignored by the social anthropologists.

The historians, on the other hand, have not always made sufficient use of the work of the social anthropologists. Since oral traditions can only be understood as part of a particular culture, it is important that the traditional historian should understand the nature and function of any oral evidence he wishes to record and interpret. It is also necessary for him to know the language of the people whose history he is studying.

It would thus appear that if we are to make good use of our oral sources, the historians and social anthropologists should co-operate in working out a methodology for using this material for historical purposes.

13 Field Work Methods in the Study of Oral Traditions in Karagwe Kingdom, Tanzania

Karagwe is one of the present-day eight kingdoms or princi-palities of West Lake Province of Tanzania. In the past, be-fore the coming of the Germans, there were only five king-doms, of which Karagwe was the largest and most powerful; the rulers of the other kingdoms were descended from sons or other relatives of one of the early kings of Karagwe. These kings are called Abahinda and are supposed to have come from Bunyoro or farther north at some time perhaps in the sixteenth century, and to have overthrown the indigenous rulers in the five kingdoms of Buhaya. Karagwe has many features of its traditional political structure in common with the kingdoms of south-western Uganda and its history is linked with Ruanda. But unlike these other kingdoms and even its Buhaya neigh-bours, the capital site in Karagwe, Bweranyange, was occupied by many generations of kings. Hence there is a considerable body of tradition concerning this area, and it is on this, on the court at Bweranyange, and on the traditional regalia that is still preserved there that my work is centred.

The material I am trying to collect concerns the origin of the kings and the indigenous political structure, the way the kings ruled and the ceremonies and events of the royal court. I have not been doing anything more than superficial work on the clan histories as this is a long and very complicated task, though these histories are part of the oral traditions of Kar-agwe. I decided to study only the history of those clans whose members had some function at the royal court or who were linked in one way or another with the kings. The actual raw material of this history consists of stories about the kings genealogical lists, songs and a form of recitation together with factual information about the historical associations of parti-cular places.

In a society like that of the Banyambo (the people of Karagwe), where there was a centralized political structure, stories about the past are linked with incidents and individuals known to the whole of the society, whereas in a society in which there is no such centralized system, the history is one of big families, as it were. It is, thus, easier to get an idea of the past of a kingdom from its traditional history than it is to get similar material where there have been neither events nor personalities linking the whole society together. In some societies with a centralized form of government there may be specialized institutions for the preservation and transmission of the traditions, such as court officials whose duty it is to remember lists of kings and stories about them, or members of certain clans who have the sole right of telling each other stories or even competitions like modern Welsh *eisteddfods* for ensuring that the traditions are remembered accurately. Where there are such formal institutions, informants will be those people who held office within the framework of one of these institutions, or members of clans in which particular traditions have been vested. In such societies it may be possible to use formal methods for the investigation and collection of material, such as sampling. But in Karagwe as far as I know no such formal institutions exist, and so it is rather a matter of talking to old men who may have worked at the royal capital, or just to those who know the old stories. The traditional history of Karagwe has been handed down from father to son by informal means such as occur in many societies throughout the world. The old men tell the stories in the evenings, reflecting on good old days. I have, therefore, found it best to work on an *ad hoc* basis, talking to those old men who are supposed to know much about the past and have consequently used informal means of collecting material.

Karagwe now comprises, and has done since European administration began, seven districts or *gombololas*. The first thing I did was to get a list of likely informants in all seven districts, from the Buhaya District Council headquarters in Karagwe.[1] I went to the Buhaya District Council Lukiko with formal letters of introduction from the administration head-

[1] The Buhaya District Council covers all eight kingdoms of Buhaya, and is what used to be called the Native Authority Administration.

quarters in Bukoba. At a meeting of the Lukiko these letters were read and I made a statement about my work, following which, a list of informants (fourteen in all with at least one from every *gombolola*) was drawn up. The Lukiko then sent letters to all the men on this list and to *gombolola* chiefs and to certain village headmen. By going round the *gombololas* in turn and asking chiefs for names of further possible informants and meeting others through field assistants, and incidentally in other informant's houses, the number gradually increased and at present I have over sixty informants. I have worked on this *ad hoc* basis of getting to know people for the reasons mentioned above and also because working from one known informant to another helps to dispel to a certain extent some of the fear and lack of trust which these old people naturally feel about an outsider and this kind of research.

It may seem a little excessive to have proceeded so formally with the Lukiko as I also did with the Tanzania African National Union officials in the area, and with both branches of the administration in order to put my work on as official a footing as possible.

There are two methods I have used in the actual collection of material; interviews with individuals, and meetings. The first method that of interviewing or talking to an individual informant is the one that I have used most often and even when I have held a meeting I later go and visit the men present in turn. A first interview usually consists of talking about what I am doing and about general topics. It is no good trying to launch into questioning at this stage as it will only antagonize informants and make things difficult later on. The most it is possible to obtain at that early stage is some idea of a genealogy, this I have found is a useful starting point as it gives something on to which to hang information and stories given later; also it is not something which is felt to be confidential and therefore not to be divulged to strangers. I found that without exception and, not surprisingly, whatever preliminaries had been made, the old men were at first very reticent and not prepared to say much. It is only after one has visited them about three or four times that they begin to trust, and only after seven or more visits that some of the more worried old men will actually offer information rather than reply to questions. A first interview usually lasts about half an hour or an hour and subsequent ones between that and two hours or, exceptionally, longer.

The method of holding meetings is satisfactory only in certain respects. So far nearly all the meetings I have held have been convened by the *gombolola* chief of an area, and I have found that though it is a quick way of getting to know the likely informants and of getting over the initial distrust, not much useful information is gathered from these meetings. Often at such a meeting one man may hold forth on some topic and the others say very little to contradict. It may be that they do not actually know the particular story in question or that they are too polite to shout the other fellow down, but so far I have not been able to get people really to discuss the controversial aspects of a story. The disadvantage of the meeting method is that, having heard a story at a meeting, a man may feel that there is nothing more to be said about it and merely repeats the story, so that it is difficult to establish whether it is a widely known story, with or without variations. Where I have held meetings I shall hold further ones when I have visited each of the individuals present several times and then can bring together all the points of difference in their statements. Another disadvantage of the meeting method is one which ties in with other difficulties in handling this traditional history. That is that much of it is regarded as confidential and especially those things which refer to sacred aspects of kingship, such as the drums, are dangerous to disclose to strangers, and when one is told about these things it is in the strictest confidence; hence a public meeting is not the best place to tackle such matters.

A few points about actual recording occur: I think it is advisable not to produce a notebook too early in an acquaintanceship as it tends to worry the old men if they think that everything is being taken down in writing. I have usually waited until I have been told by the informant to write things down or until it was otherwise clear that it would not worry him. Apart from recording what is actually said in the course of an interview, I also make a note of the time of the interview, the place, and the people present during it. I think this is significant in assessing the information; one is told different things in informal situations, such as sitting round a fire in the evening when there is no need to worry about getting out into the *shamba* to do some work, than in situations when strangers or children from other families are present, when it is sometimes not possible to have anything other than a general conversation. I have found no difficulty at all in the use of a tape recorder. This I have not used for getting down straightforward information, or even stories, as it is better to try to write these down and then one pays more attention to the content and asks questions about points in the story. I have used the tape recorder for recording songs and the heroic recitations but have either at the same time or at a later stage also got down the words of these. These songs incidentally require a great deal of interpretation and it is dangerous just to let the machine do all the work as one can end up with a fine collection of stuff but not knowing what it is all about. Most people have enjoyed listening to themselves on the tape and, though at first I was afraid to use it too soon, I have since found that it is a good way of breaking the ice and that often after a recording session other information is volunteered. The only minor drawback is that word gets round about the machine and one tends to have to record a great deal of useless material just for the sake of public relations. It has seemed at times that half a village has turned up in a man's house to talk to the 'mashini'.

At meetings, as in the interviews, I have adopted no formal procedure; rather, I thought it better to allow informants to volunteer what they wished and not try to keep to any pattern of questioning, which on the other hand might help with the comparison of statements. I have kept to certain probes and methods of questioning but these have always been used to fit in with the conversation and not according to some kind of questionnaire. I said that in a first interview I very often asked for genealogical material and for the names of the kings; in subsequent interviews when there has been no spontaneous offering of information I have used probes such as: 'I have heard that there was a king called such and such; what did he do? who was his father? etc.' Or I have asked vague questions about what Karagwe was like in the past, how big it was, who lived there on so on. In later interviews I have also used another method which is to make out that one knows a fair amount about a topic anyhow; that one is no novice and that one would simply like to know about a few of the finer points. This sort of thing has been especially helpful in tackling the question of drums and other mystical aspects of kingship. I ought to add that in this connexion it is more than a help to know the language. It goes without saying that contact is easier and better with people when you can speak to them in their own language even if with the help of an interpreter at times, but if one wishes to show off, it is only effective in the vernacular. Apart from making for easier contact the informal interview has also other advantages. Although there are certain obvious questions one can ask I have also found that very many lines of approach are suggested by points that crop up incidentally in interviews and if a more rigid pattern of interviewing was adhered to, these would be lost. For example, it is stated in Speke and in subsequent books (e.g. by Cory) that the capital of Karagwe was and always has been Bweranyange. Quite incidentally one of my informants started talking about a tree-stump (*akasibo ka nyina Ntare* in the village of Karagwe: which is supposed to mark the spot where the wife of the first king of Karagwe rested, (or gave birth), when she was pregnant. On asking others I found that many think the village of Karagwe was the first capital of Karagwe and in fact the place which gave the name to the whole kingdom.

A further point about the value of information volunteered, rather than given in reply to questions, is that it is very difficult to pose questions which are not angled and suggest an answer. One knows what one is trying to find out and the danger is that one puts a convenient answer into the informant's mouth. Also I think that many feel they have to produce an answer to a question and in my experience the Banyambo are not lacking in imagination or sense of humour. I asked one man what a particular clan did at Bweranyange and was told that they looked after the drum and other regalia (which is true according to other statements) but that they also took the thorns out of the feet of any lions which happened to frequent the royal compound. And there are many other such highly colourful inventions I am offered and which are not supported by other statements, and which may well have been produced because the man felt he ought to provide an answer.

There are several more aspects of actual methods of collecting material which I shall cover. First the use of an assistant. I have used several and now have an excellent Standard 10 boy[1] who helps with language, with finding people and with collecting some of the background information about informants. It is a great help to have an assistant; I have met several most knowledgeable informants through him, and in the actual collection of material it speeds up interviews and avoids aggravating people if one has someone to explain what has been said when one does not understand rather than slowly having to puzzle it out oneself. He can also frame questions quickly, again avoiding too much delay. But it is dangerous to rely on an assistant and not to know any of the language; it is quite easy and not a matter of deceit for him to give explanations of a reply rather than a straightforward translation and if one knew nothing of what had been said it would be impossible to detect this. The same is true of framing questions; one must know enough to be able to understand that he does not put answers into the heads of the informants.

The second matter concerns the amount of time one should spend in an area. With seven districts to cover it has been quite easy to spend about a week in a district and then move to another. For a variety of reasons I have not gone systematically all round and then started again at the beginning, but rather have worked in one group of districts returning to each one at an interval of some two to three weeks; and then leaving that group for a longer period to work on the other group. The reason for not sitting down for longer in any one district is that I felt there was a limit to the number of times one could go and ask questions in a short space of time. I think that when one has only about six or seven people to see in a district one cannot reasonably worry them more than two or three times in a week. A week or so is long enough in one *gombolola*. I may be mistaken in this and certainly it may have no relevance to other areas but I have felt that this was the best way to avoid informants feeling that the meeting was a daily suffering.

And then, lastly, there is the question of payment of informants. I feel that payment in cash is rather dangerous as it may well lead to the manufacture of information; I am sure that for ten shillings many a Munyambo could make up an

---

[1] Standard 10 is the top form of the Middle or Junior Secondary School.

excellent and clever piece of traditional history. But on the other hand one must repay the kindness and help and patience which informants (certainly nearly all of mine) have shown. Instead of money, I take small presents like tobacco, coffee, tea and sugar; if meat is given, one first must find out about taboos. Many, in fact most, of these old men are poor and infirm and welcome gifts; and it is quite in keeping with Bahaya custom to take a present on such occasions, even though the most usual form of giving is when one visits rather than one is visited. Another easy way of repaying help, is to buy beer of which all old Banyambo—and young too for that matter—are fond. But that can only be at a beer party when there is beer available, as it would certainly be considered rather odd to go about with large gourds of beer ready to dispense to helpful informants. As with money payments, gifts have to be given with care otherwise they might turn into bribes and again invite the manufacture of material.

I mentioned earlier that as well as finding traditional history about people and incidents, one must also look for places which have some kind of historical association; and then it is a matter of going to see people who live where a lineage or sometimes a larger kin group has always been attached to a particular area. A few examples in Karagwe will illustrate what I mean.

Fairly early on in this study I heard about a village not far from Bweranyange to which the kings were afraid to go. On going there I found that the members of this village were nearly all of one clan and that the clan was responsible for the making and guarding of the royal drums. There is a great deal of mystique surrounding the drums and in that village there is a sort of knot of traditions about drums and the reverence of the king for them. The reason why the king fears to go there is that these clansfolk 'know more than the king'; they know what mystical thing was put inside the drum when it was made, and because they play the drum, they can 'walk in front of the king'.

Then in another village live members of another clan which has the sole right of playing *amakondere*, the trumpet-like instrument which is always played on special royal occasions, such as the ceremonies which were traditionally held at the beginning of the month. Here again there is a cluster of traditions about the playing of *amakondere* which are not found elsewhere.

Again in Bugara in the north of Karagwe lives another clan to which the indigenous king Nono, who was overthrown by the first Hinda king, belonged. Here the traditions about that king and his fall from power are better known than elsewhere.

It goes without saying that in and around the capital of Bweranyange, and in the villages near the place where all the kings are supposed to be buried there are local pockets of tradition. It is then very important to follow up all the leads that one may obtain about historical places.

I shall end by giving an illustration of the kind of story that constitutes traditional history and which is of the sort that I at least am looking for and recording. I shall give two of many versions of the many stories which account for the disappearance of a mysterious group of half-human, half-spirit kings from whom some people say the kings of Karagwe, and those of other western lacustrine kingdoms, are descended. One of these Abacwezi, as these kings are called, was Wamara.

These two stories are more or less as they were given to me, which will, I hope, give some idea of the way in which they are told as well as an idea of the content of such stories. It will be seen that though the two versions differ in some and perhaps important details (for example the colour of the cow) essentially they tell the same tale. This is not the place to go into an analysis of the meaning of the story or of the social significance of its contents, but I shall just draw attention to one feature of these and many other stories about kings: the importance of cattle.

Wamara had a lot of children, and when they were grown into men he gave them each a country to rule. He also killed those who did bad and they were changed into spirits or *abacwezi*. Wamara was especially fond of one of his grandsons called Kagoro. Wamara had a house and in that house he kept a beautiful cow which nobody saw. It was a brown cow and nobody ever saw it and it never went out of the house, but just stayed there and made Wamara very happy when he saw it. It was called *Bihogo bya rutwenge* (which means that which pleased him). Wamara brought it grass but it did not eat ordinary grass like other cows. Then one day Kagoro's uncles came and they said that they wanted to see the cow. So Kagoro who was so loved by his grandfather went and joked with the old man and said he wanted to build a house on top of his grandfather's. And this the grandfather allowed. And then Kagoro went and slept in the house when it was ready. Another day he went to Wamara and said that he wanted to burn down his new house. But his grandfather was not pleased because he knew his house would burn too. But Wamara loved Kagoro and so the house was burnt down. Then Wamara went into the burning house to take out the lovely cow and as he did so the uncles saw the cow. And as the cow had never been in the sun before, it didn't know about it and it was too hot and so it fell down and died. Wamara was very angry at this and punished them all by making them and himself sink into the ground. Even those sons who were in other parts sank into the ground and that was the last that was heard of them and how they all became spirits or *abacwezi*.

And this is another version of the story:

Wamara had a cow which was white and it was called *ekitare kya Wamara*. This cow did not eat grass but *eshisha* (big round straw) and nobody could look at the *eshisha* or at the cow. Wamara did not want even his sons and his wife Nyamutwe to see the cow. Then one day Kagoro kya Chomya and Isimbwa who were grandsons of Wamara wanted to look at the cow and at Wamara's wife. They said they wanted to build houses inside their grandfather's house. And as their grandfather loved them very much, he allowed them to do this. Then after they had built the house they decided that they wanted to burn it, but their grandfather was angry. Even so they burnt down the two houses and the cow and Wamara's wife came out and the flies bit the cow and it died, and Isimbwa took the woman by force. At this Wamara was furious and consulted a diviner called Nyakoka who looked at the insides of two cows and found no heart or internal organs, and he said that this meant that it was the end of the kingdom of Wamara.

14 Place Names, Proverbs, Idioms and Songs as a Check on Traditional History

The Baganda are fortunate in that for about five centuries they have been able to build up a traditional history undisturbed by invasion, with its attendant sacking and pillaging of the royal tombs and temples. On the death of each of the thirty-two kings of the present dynasty in Buganda a princess (*Nalinnya*) was appointed as the custodian of the history and achievements of the dead king, and by consulting these traditions it has been possible to obtain a fairly comprehensive account of the intrigues and exploits of the clan leaders and priests who influenced the affairs of Buganda during each reign.

Unfortunately, there appears to be little left to us of the temple traditions, with the exception of the *Kibaale* of Kkungu, who happened to be both a priest and a clan leader and who, in 1820, had to plead his case before *Kabaka* Kamaanya and so had the history of his clan and deity enshrined with that of Kamaanya, to be recorded by Sir Apolo Kagwa less than eighty years later. With this exception, the zeal of the Baganda is sweeping away all traces of the pagan past.

As a result of the conversion of most Baganda to Christianity and Islam, the keepers of the temple traditions died without passing on their lore. Or if a few morsels were passed on, they are furtively hidden from anyone who might try and record them.

By the time the present dynasty of Buganda was set up by Kimera, the Lwoo clansmen who accompanied him had already been in contact with Bantu culture in Bunyoro–Kitara some two hundred years. To the princesses who had to decide what details were to be memorized as oral tradition, details of the weapons of Kimera's followers, of what they ate and how they were dressed, (which would today be some guide to us in determining how quickly they became integrated with the general population), seemed trivial compared to the names and clans of the royal wives and of the senior chiefs and the wars which took place during the reign of their royal charges.

Here and there something of the social life of the people has, however, been preserved and we are fortunate in that *Kabaka* Jjuuko, the fourteenth in succession after Kimera, must have had a more imaginative *Nalinnya* than most of the others, and so there is much more detail about the people who served him handed down to us from Bujuuko, where he is buried. This is not all; for very strongly emphasized in the Bujuuko traditions is the description of a total eclipse of the sun which took place and which was observed at Wagaba and Bakka. The eclipse has been ascertained to have occurred on the 30 March 1680. Another more serious matter was the first appearance of bubonic plague in Buganda, of which Jjuuko died.

We are told that when, in the past, a *Kabaka* wished to have wives, the clan elders would bring the most comely of the unmarried girls to the palace and they thus became recognized as wives of the *Kabaka*. From the Jjuuko stories it would seem that this was not always so, for a story, which also tells us about the naming of the hill on which Uganda's University College is built, indicates that the *Kabaka* could go in person to pay court to anyone whose beauty had been extolled before him. The girl in this case was Nalunga, who lived at Nabutitti. The royal party had set off before dawn to go and visit her and their route took them over Makerere, which they reached just as the sun was rising. Jjuuko stopped to admire the beauty of the scene and remarked that they had made an early start (*gano gabadde makeerere*). From this chance remark the hill was renamed Makeerere (early start hill), and so it is pronounced to this day. Unfortunately, the first surveyor to mark it on a map was unaware of the subtlety of the name and wrote it down as Makerere, by which mutilation it would seem all future generations must abide.

Jjuuko married Nalunga and she became his favourite wife, her fame spreading all over the kingdom, but alas, even she nearly fell from grace through going too far in her endeavours to please her lord. One of Jjuuko's favourite dishes was *mugoye*, a mixture of sweet potatoes and beans mashed together into a kind of cake. Nalunga thought she could improve on this by substituting coco yams for the sweet potatoes, but Jjuuko did not appreciate the mixture and she was probably lucky to escape with her life. The Baganda remember the event by the idiom: *Nkole mpoomye, Nalunga yagoya amayuuni.* (Let me try and please, poor Nalunga tried to make mugoye with coco yams.) It is also recorded that the name of the hill, Bukasa, where Nalunga tried out her culinary skill had its name changed to Nkolempoomye.

What is important about this story is that by 1680 the sweet potato appears to have been established in Buganda, although it may have been something of a novelty. The coco yam was obviously an older food and so the *Kabaka* did not take kindly to 'peasant food' in the form of the yam.

Before Kimera came to Buganda there had been rulers such as Katonda, Buganda, Bbemba Musota and, most famous of them all and considered to be the maker of Buganda, Kintu. At Nkono in Busujju there is a shrine where the exploits of Kintu and his heaven-born wife, Nambi Nantuttululu are remembered. Kintu was probably the same person as the Isaza Waraga Nyakikooto of the traditions of Bunyoro-Kitara and Nambi, the daughter of heaven, would correspond to the fabulous Nyamate, daughter of the king of the underworld in the Runyoro and Runyankore versions.

Kintu met Nambi when she strayed from heaven and got her ear caught and injured in a snare he had set (hence the name *Nantuttululu*—deformed ear). He was then but a simple pastoralist and hunter, but he not only accepted Nambi's love and help, but also her advice on how to till the soil, and so became an agriculturist. She took him to visit her father in heaven, who gave them his blessing and told them to hurry back to earth before Nambi's jealous brother, Death, discovered that Kintu had taken Nambi to Earth. Unfortunately, on their way back, Nambi remembered that she had left some millet seed behind, and turned back to fetch it. Thus she met Death, who trailed her to Earth and has since taken his toll of Kintu's children.

This story indicates that when Buganda was in the making the Baganda were millet eaters, a food more suitable to warriors and nation-builders than the plantain which has today supplanted it. The findings of the dieticians on the deficiencies of a plantain diet would suggest that the Baganda would never have risen to the commanding position which they held 100 years ago had plantains been their main food, and it could also be suggested that it is the increasing use of the plantain and beer banana which have caused the Baganda to lose the advantages of the predominant place they were given by the spread outwards from Buganda of Christianity, Islam and the British Administration, which took with them the attendant advantage of educational and economic development.

Apart from the Kintu tradition about millet, there is a little song which has been sung by Baganda children over the ages, which is:

> *Ssekiso, Ssekiso, tonseeraako obulo?*
> *Naakuseeraako obulo, laba bwe nsaako.*

The song represents a child who is not old enough to have her grindstone asking a skilled grinder if he will please grind her some millet. Ssekiso, the skilled grinder, replies that he cannot do so because he already has a number of commissions to fulfil.

There is a Luganda proverb *mpola, mpola eyisa obusera* meaning more haste, less speed, which refers to the cooking of *obusera*, a gruel made from millet. Modern idiom has taken this further and will euphemistically refer to a glass of whisky or brandy as *otusera*. Thus a whisky-drinking Muganda will call for his drink in such terms and at the same time stoutly deny that the Baganda were ever millet eaters and will say that Nambi turned back to fetch the millet because she wanted it to feed to her chickens. Anyone who knows the tedious process of growing and harvesting millet will realize that the last thing anyone would do would be to grow it as chicken feed. It was cultivated because it was a tasty, storable, nourishing food more easy to transport than the yam and quickly grown, for two crops could be harvested in a year. Nature herself helped with determining when the sowing of the millet was to take place, for this coincided with the season when the nightjar came out in heavy breeding plumage. At night the husbandman would listen for the whistle of the nightjar in flight and know that the time to sow was at hand. The Runyoro name for the nightjar is *orutambaisiga*, meaning the foreteller of the sowing season.

In Butambala, only forty miles from Kampala, is a trading

centre shown on the maps as Bulo. In fact it is called Mu Bulo, indicating that it was once the centre of an area in which millet was extensively grown, just as Mu Kisenyi indicates an area from which sand may be taken, or Mu Kiwafu indicates an area where the wild plum may be had in abundance.

Other place names which show that the Baganda recognized the importance of the grindstone or quern are Kammengo and Mmengo. Mmengo is the plural of *lubengo*, a grindstone. The present seat of the Buganda Government owes its name to the fact that the Baganda went there to quarry the granite blocks on the hill, and not, as some wag has suggested, to ascertain whether the Mills of God ground any faster there than in Entebbe. Not far from Entebbe is another place name, Sisa, which means 'I do not grind'.

There are three main species of yam known to the Baganda: the coco yam which is grown on swampy land, the climbing yam which goes under the general name of *mmere y'omu ttaka*, meaning the food hidden in the soil, and lastly the *nnumbu*, a small, delicately flavoured, potato-like plant which, like the millet, is a tedious crop to grow and harvest, and so has today vanished from the scene not only in Buganda but in Tooro, although it was being grown in the latter area fifteen years ago. The huge increase in the cultivation of the plantain which the last fifty years has seen in Tooro, has forced the *nnumba* out in the same way as it was forced out of Buganda by the settled conditions brought about during the reigns of Ssuuna and Muteesa I.

Eight miles from Kampala, near Kaazi and Bulingugwe Island, is a hill called Zzirannumbu, meaning the place which will not grow *nnumba* yams. This hill is mentioned in the traditions concerning the one *Kabaka* of Buganda whom the Baganda are ready to admit went too far in the tyrannous treatment he meted out to his subjects: Kagulu Tebuucwereke. Kagulu went too far when he ordered the execution of the head of the Monkey Clan, *Mugema*. The original *Mugema* had saved the infant Kimera from a clay pit into which, like Moses in the Bible story, the child had been cast, and Kimera had exhorted all future kings of Buganda that the *Mugema* was never to have a spear pointed at him, he could not be executed, and was to be treated as if he was the father of the *Kabaka*.

This was the first time in 250 years that a *Mugema* had been touched, and the Baganda revolted against Kagulu, led by a princess called Ndege, whose brother had been killed by Kagulu. Ndege harried Kagulu to and fro until Kagulu, passing over Zzirannumbu hill, took refuge on Bulingugwe Island and found a canoe to take him across to the Kojja Peninsula. Here the relentless Ndege tracked him down and drowned him in a murky pool by the lake shore.

In Kagulu's day, which was about the beginning of the eighteenth century and some twenty years after Jjuuko's death, the *nnumba* yam was being cultivated in Buganda. In fact here and there one may today find an old Muganda who remembers having eaten the *nnumbu*.

In his *Comprehensive Study of the Bantu and Semi-Bantu Languages*, Sir Harry Johnston pointed out that whereas the Lacustrine Bantu used the word *nte* for cattle, their neighbours used either *inka* or *ngombe*. Furthermore, the word for milk outside the Lacustrine Bantu area was the same as the word for breasts: *mabeere* or *maziwa*. Among the Lacustrine Bantu *mabeere* means breasts, but for milk the word is either *mate* or *mata*. Bugisu and Rwanda are just on the fringe of the Lacustrine Bantu. In Bugisu a cow is *inkafu* and milk is *maveeri*; Runyarwanda compromises with *inka* for a cow and *mata* for milk.

The Lacustrine Bantu have taken the stem *-te* and prefixed *n-* for the animal and *ma-* for the milk it produces, furthermore, when the Muhima wants to talk about herds of cattle he refers to them as *masyo*, and so does the Mutuutsi. The Muganda, however, reverts to the basic Bantu word *magana* when referring to herds of cattle.

There seems to be evidence that the words for cattle and milk as used by the Baganda, Banyoro, Basoga and others have come from the Southern Sudan, and furthermore can be related to the Masai, as the following comparative vocabulary list will show:

	Singular	Plural
Kakwa	*kite*	*su*
Bari	*Kiteng*	*kisuk*
Teso	*akiteng*	*aituk*
Karamojong	*ate*	*ngatuk*

	Singular	Plural
Toposa	*aiteng*	*ngaituk*
Masai	*giteng*	*gishu*
Lugbara and Madi	*ti*	*ti*
Acooli	*dyang*	*dyang*

When driving cattle the Munyoro herdsman will shout: *Hasuka*! and when he is ready to water them he will call out *Eresu, eresu*. He cannot explain the meaning of the words, but the cattle, through constant usage, understand them perfectly well.

In Luganda the words *nte* and *mata* are used for cattle and milk in folklore, songs, idioms and proverbs, and so can be regarded as having been absorbed thoroughly into the language, but there do not appear to be very many place names with the stem *nte* in them. One hill, Kiringente, near the former temple of the god of war, Kibuuka, has a story to account for it. There are several perched granite boulders on it and tradition has it that one day Kabaka Jjunju was out hunting in the vicinity and from where he was, the perched boulders looked like a cow, so he remarked: *kiri ng'ente* (it looks like a cow), and so from that day the hill's former name was abandoned and Kiringente it became.

In Kampala there is a small stream which runs through a valley separating the granites of Nakaseero from the dolerite intruded schists and quartzites of Kololo. The earth eroded from the two hills has formed a particularly clastic type of clay, and any cattle unfortunate enough to get bogged down in it were likely to perish, so it was named the Kittante, or killer of cattle.

Two places called Ntenjeru (the white cow) come to mind: one in Bugerere and one in Kyaggwe. A place name similarly compounded is Nkokonjeru (the white hen) and it is possible that this name is of comparatively recent derivation. Semei Kakunguru's naming of that foothill of Mount Elgon near Mbale is certainly of recent origin and so is the Nkokonjeru in Mbarara, where the Mugabe Kahaya is buried.

The Bukalasa Farm Institute is only thirty-two miles out of Kampala, but its name shows that the Banyoro once lived here, since it is made up of the diminutive prefix *bu-*, the Runyoro past tense infix -*ka*- and the stem -*lasa*, meaning shoot. It appears to refer to an occasion when some band of 'contemptibles' made such good use of their skill as archers that the enemy was put to flight. Doubtless the enemy were the Baganda, pushing outwards from the Bbombo area towards the marches of Bunyoro–Kitara. A Bukalasa also occurs in Buddu, an area conquered from the Banyoro as late as 1780 by *Kabaka* Jjunju.

Tables

Epoch	Years	Hominid / Primate	Stone Age	Industry	Locality	Remarks
PLEISTOCENE — MIDDLE	300,000	'Chellean man' *Homo erectus pithecanthropus*	EARLY STONE AGE	ACHEULEAN / CHELLEAN } Handaxe industries — Hope Fountain variant	Nsongezi, Uganda; Olorgesailie, Kenya; Kariandusi, Kenya; Isimila, Tanganyika; Olduvai, Beds III–IV	Full development of handaxe industries. Some Gigantic animal species found at Olduvai and Olorgesailie
PLEISTOCENE — LOWER	1,500,000	*Homo habilis* and '*Zinjanthropus*'			Olduvai Bed II	First spread of Man into Europe and Asia
	— 3,000,000 —			OLDOWAN 'Chopping tools'	Olduvai Gorge, Tanganyika, and lower part Bed II; Bed I	The HUMAN REVOLUTION, transition from scavenging to hunting. First systematic stone-toolmaking
			STANDARDIZED TOOLS			
PLIOCENE	— 14,000,000 —	*Kenyapithecus wickeri* ? Miocene			Fort Ternan, Kenya	Only discovery so far—jaw fragments. Period probably saw the development of fully bipedal primates
MIOCENE	15,000,000 —	GENUS PROCONSUL *P. major* *P. nyanzae*			Kavirondo area of Kenya; Moroto, Uganda; Rusinga, Kenya	Emergence of partially bipedal primates
	30,000,000 —					

TABLE 1. STONE AGE CULTURES OF EAST AFRICA

Geological Period	Years B.C.	Human and Pre-human Types	Human Cultures	Most Important Sites	Remarks
PLEISTOCENE					
	0	*Homo sapiens*	MIDDLE STONE AGE / LATER STONE AGE		
		→ Spread of Bantu-speaking peoples	Beginning of Iron Age	Nsongezi rock shelter Uganda	Spread of agriculture into sub-Saharan Africa
	1,000		TSHITOLIAN		? Beginnings of rock paintings
	4,000	Bushmanoid peoples	LUPEMBAN II — WILTON		First bows and arrows Specialized fishing communities
	10,000	Development of present African races	KENYA CAPSIAN — MAGOSIAN	Ishango, Congo Magosi, Uganda Gambles Cave, Kenya (Capsian)	
UPPER	20,000		LUPEMBAN I — STILLBAY	Nsongezi erosion gullies, Uganda	First indications of burials, Caucasoid elements entering East Africa from Horn of Africa
	30,000	Rhodesoid races	→ SANGOAN — FAURESMITH	Gitgil river, Kenya (Stillbay)	Development of stone tipped missiles (lances, etc.)
	60,000		SPECIALIZED TOOLS / COMPOSITE TOOLS	Sango Bay, Uganda Mount Kenya (Fauresmith)	Use of caves for habitation begins; discovery of fire and new toolmaking techniques (e.g. prepared core) leads to Man's greater adaptability

Date	Event	Source	Date notes
Early 13th century	Pate Sultanate founded. First mention of Unguja (town on Zanzibar island) and Malindi	Pate Chronicle	Date unreliable
Late 13th–14th century	Kilwa controls Sofala; monumental buildings at Kilwa with introduction of vaults. Gedi, Kilepwa, Ungwana in existence; Mogadishu flourishes	Kilwa Chronicle; archaeological	First substantial imports Chinese Porcelain. Beads mainly of wound type
1332	Names of Sultan of Kilwa and successor as in Chronicle confirmed. Makonde–Makua peoples at Kilwa?	Ibn Battuta's visit	Main period of coining, Kilwa.
Late 14th century	Pate in ascendent	Pate Chronicle	Authenticity of Pate's conquests very doubtful
15th century	Flowering of towns on Kenya Coast. Pillar Tombs, c. 1430 reconstruction of Great Mosque at Kilwa—Indian influence?	Archaeological	Islamic monochrome pottery imported
End of 15th century	Mombasa in ascendant; Kilwa's power waning.	Kilwa Chronicle Portuguese sources	Coins minted in Mogadishu and Zanzibar
1498	Vasco da Gama's voyage to India	Portuguese sources	
1505	Portuguese overrun Kilwa and Mombasa. Main base at Malindi. Rapid decline of coast, especially southern part	Portuguese sources	
1569	Kilwa almost deserted	Fr. Monclaro	
Late 16th century	Galla move south	Traditions; archaeological evidence, Gedio	
1592	Invasion of Zimba		
1593	Portuguese station moves to Mombasa; building of Fort Jesus		
1612	First account of route into interior (Kilwa to Zambezi)	Boccaro	
Late 17th century	Omanis attack in East Africa		Greatest period of building at Zimbabwe
1698	Fall of Fort Jesus. End of Portuguese domination		

TABLE 2. CHRONOLOGICAL SCHEME OF HISTORY OF EAST AFRICAN COAST

Date A.D.	Events	Evidence	Remarks
2nd century, and probably earlier	Arab and Graeco-Roman trade with East African Coast. Rhapta under King of S.W. Arabia. Arabs intermarry with (? Hamitic) inhabitants of Coast	Periplus of Erythraean Sea	No material objects found of period
622	Beginning of Islamic era in Arabia		
Late 7th-early 8th century	Immigration of Shias	Annals of Oman (18th cent.) De Barros (16th cent.	Authenticity somewhat doubtful
Late 7th century	Immigration of 'Syrians'	Chronicles of Lamu and Pate; Kitab al-Zanuj (all recent redactions)	Mythical?
Second half of 8th century	Coast overrun and governed by Abbasid Caliphs	Kitab al-Zanuj	Mythical?
9th century or later	Earliest identified settlements on coast (Unguja, Ukuu, Kilwa, possibly others).	Archaeological	
9th century	Refugees from near al-Hasa (W. side Persian Gulf) settle at Mogadishu and Barawa	De Barros (16th cent.)	Perhaps duplication of 'Shirazi' immigration
916	Al-Masudi visits Kanbalu (? Pemba, ? Madagascar) which is Muslim. First mention of Sofala. Bantu already on coast	al-Masudi; also Buzurg ibn Shahriyar	
Late 10th century (traditional date but more probably 12th century).	Immigration from Persian Gulf ('Shirazis') settling at Pemba, Mafia, Kilwa and elsewhere. Beginning of Kilwa sultanate	Kilwa Chronicle	First coins? Coursed masonry at Kilwa
12th century	Kisimani Mafia an important town (and probably earlier also). First stone buildings at Zimbabwe. Gold trade becomes important	Archaeological	
	Malindi and Mombasa in existence	Al-Idrisi	
1107	Earliest known inscription (Kizimkazi)		

Selected Reading

This list is only of preliminary and easily accessible references mostly in English. Most of the references contain full lists of further books and articles. Particularly extensive and useful lists can be found in the following two books:

OLIVER, R. & MATHEW, G.	*A History of East Africa*, vol. I (1963).
COLE, SONIA	*The Pre-history of East Africa* (1963), for books and journal references on pre-history.

The following Journals all contain useful articles from time to time on East Africa:

> *The Journal of African History*
> *The South African Archaeological Bulletin*
> *The Uganda Journal*
> *Tanganyika Notes and Records*
> *Proceedings* of the first four pan-African Pre-history Congresses held in 1947, 1952, 1955 and 1959 and published in 1952, 1955, 1957 and 1962 respectively. (1952 and 1959 Proceedings published in France and Belgium respectively.)

General Books

CLARK, J. G. D.	*Archaeology and Society* (London, 1959).
	World Pre-history (London, 1960).
OLIVER R. (*ed.*)	*The Dawn of African History* (London, 1960).
CLARK, J. D.	*The Pre-history of Southern Africa* (London, 1959).
DAVIDSON, B.	*Old Africa Re-discovered* (London, 1959).
OLIVER, R. & FAGE, J. D.	*A Short History of Africa* (London, 1962).
LEAKEY, L. S. B.	*Adam's Ancestors* (London, 1953).
BROTHWELL, D. & HIGGS, E. S.	*Science in Archaeology* (London, 1963).

Part 1

HUMAN EVOLUTION AND THE STONE AGES

For the Geological background the following are recommended:

BISHOP, W. W. & POSNANSKY, M.	'Pleistocene Environments and Early Man in Uganda', *Uganda Journal*, vol. 24 (1960), pp. 44–62.

ZEUNER, F.   *Dating the Past*, London, 1957 ed. (discusses
                     most of the problems of dating but now rather
                     out of date).

CURTISS, G. H.   in *National Geographic Magazine*, October
                     1961, pp. 590–2 (for potassium argon dating).

COOKE, H. B. S.   'Observations Relating to Quaternary Envir-
                     onments in East and Southern Africa', *du Toit
                     Memorial Lecture 5 of the Geological Society
                     of South Africa* (1959), p. 73.

FLINT, R. F.   'Pleistocene Climates in Eastern and Southern
                     Africa', *Bull. Geol. Soc. of America*, vol. 70
                     (1959), pp. 343–374.

MORRISON, M. E. S.   'Pollen analysis in Uganda', *Nature*, vol. 190
                     (1961), pp. 483–6 (the only detailed account of
                     pollen analytical work in East Africa).

The Natural Resources of East Africa, E. W. RUSSELL (ed.) (Nairobi,
1962) contains brief accounts of the present-day environment of
East Africa with excellent specially drawn maps.

On aspects of human evolution, W. LE GROS CLARK, *The Antecedents of Man* (London, 1960); ARDREY, ROBERT *African Genesis*
(London, 1961) and HOWELLS, W. W. *Mankind in the Making*
(London, 1959) are the most valuable, supplemented for East Africa
by LEAKEY, L. S. B., *'The Progress and Evolution of Man in Africa*
(Oxford, 1961) and articles in the *National Geographic Magazine* for
1960, vol. 118, pp. 420–35; 1961, vol. 120, pp. 564–90 and 1963,
vol. 123, pp. 132–52.

For the Earlier Stone Age the reader is best advised to refer firstly
to two books dealing with the making of stone tools, OAKLEY, K. P.
Man the Toolmaker, British Museum Guide, 4th ed. (1958), and
KNOWLES, SIR FRANCIS H. S. *The Stone-worker's Progress* (1953), Pitt-
Rivers Museum, Occasional Papers on Technology, No. 6.

Few books have appeared on the whole of the Stone Age except
for LEAKEY, L. S. B. *Stone Age Africa* (London, 1936) (now largely
out of date) and ALIMEN, H. *The Prehistory of Africa* (London, 1957).

For Uganda the Stone Age sequence is in part summarized in
BISHOP and POSNANSKY, *op. cit.* Most of the Stone Age is covered by
individual excavation reports, the most important of which are:
LEAKEY, L. S. B., *Olduvai Gorge* (Cambridge, 1951) (now out of date
though a new monograph is in the press of which the first part only
has appeared) which deals with the Early Stone Age sequence.

LEAKEY, L. S. B., *Stone Age Cultures of Kenya Colony* (Cambridge, 1931) provides the classic, though out of date, sequence of Stone Age cultures of Kenya; it is of value particularly for the account of the excavations at Kariandusi and Gambles Cave. O'BRIEN, T. P., *The Prehistory of Uganda* (Cambridge, 1939) provides a similar account of excavations in Uganda, particularly in the Kagera Valley and at several cave sites.

LOWE, C. H. VAN RIET, *The Pleistocene Geology and Prehistory of Uganda*, Part II, Geological Survey of Uganda, Memoir. No. 6 (1952) Covers the work done by Wayland at Nsongezi before the war and describes several Sangoan sites.

HEINZELIN, J. DE BRAUCOURT, *Les Fouilles d'Ishango* (Institut des Parcs Nationaux du Congo Belge, Brussels, 1957) provides an account of the important Late Stone Age excavations at Ishango on Lake Albert and with ARKELL, A. J. *Early Khartoum* (Oxford, 1949) gives detailed descriptions of two sites where fishing communities developed.

No account of all the rock-paintings of East Africa has been published though the following provide regional summaries: for Uganda, POSNANSKY, M., Rock Paintings on Lolui Island, *Uganda Journal*, vol. 25 (1961), pp. 105–11; for Kenya, WRIGHT, R., 'A Painted Rock Shelter on Mount Elgon, Kenya', *Proceedings of the Prehistoric Society*, vol. 28 (1961), pp. 28–35, and for Tanganyika, 'Rock Paintings in Tanganyika', *Tanganyika Notes and Records*, No. 29 (1950). For an account of techniques of recording and the problems of interpretation LHOTE, H., *The Search for the Tassili Frescoes* (London, 1960) provides an exciting beginning. WILLCOX, A. R., *Rock Paintings of the Drakensburg* (London, 1956); *The Rock Art of South Africa* (1963) and *Rock Art of Central Africa* (1959) (*ed.* R. SUMMERS for the National Publications Trust Rhodesia and Nyasaland), provide excellent illustrated surveys of the rock paintings and engravings of Southern Africa.

Part 2

THE PEOPLING OF AFRICA AND THE FOUNDATIONS OF AFRICAN SOCIETY

On crop origins and language the most up-to-date accounts are contained in a series of papers in the *Journal of African History*, Part 2 (1962) and MURDOCK, G. P., *Africa, Its Peoples and their Culture History* (New York, 1959). ZEUNER, F. E., *A History of Domesticated Animals* (London, 1963) has an excellent bibliography though it covers the topic from a world aspect.

For general aspects of agriculture and a bibliography, COBLEY, L. S., *An Introduction to the Botany of Tropical Crops* (London, 1956) is a valuable source.

Other important articles on agricultural origins are: BRAIDWOOD, R. J., *Courses towards Urban Life* (1962, Viking Fund Publications in Anthropology, No. 32, New York), a series of essays dealing in part with the transition from a hunter-foodgatherer to a food-producing economy.

MCMASTER, D. N., 'Some Speculations on the Coming of the Banana to Uganda', *Uganda Journal*, vol. 27 (1963), pp. 163–75, contains a geographical approach to the problem of the spread of the banana.

POSNANSKY, M., 'Bantu Genesis', *Uganda Journal*, vol. 25 (1961), pp. 86–93.

SAUER, C. O., *Agricultural Origins and Dispersals* (New York, 1952; American Geographical Society, 1952) presents an account of the origins of agriculture in South East Asia and its spread from there westwards.

On cattle origins the three most informative accounts, which both contain full bibliographies, are:

MASON, I. L., & J. P. MAULE, *The Indigenous Livestock of Eastern and Southern Africa* (Commonwealth Agricultural Bureaux, London, 1960).

FAULKNER, P. E., & H. EPSTEIN, *The Indigenous Cattle of the British Dependent Territories in Africa*, publication of the Colonial Council for Agriculture Animal Health and Forestry. No. 5 (London, 1957).

PAYNE, W. J. A., The Origin of Domestic Cattle in Africa, *Empire Journal of Experimental Agriculture*, vol. 32 (1964), pp. 97–113.

On language few books have been written which provide a general introduction to the subject:

GREENBERG, J., *The Languages of Africa* (The Hague, 1963) is the only up-to-date attempt at a classification and contains a bibliography.

SELIGMAN, C. G., *The Races of Africa*, 3rd ed. (Oxford, 1957) which is a classic book on the subject, is out of date but is useful as an historical outline of the present nomenclature as normally used.

No books on physical aspects have been produced and most of the papers are in inaccessible medical and specialist journals.

COON, C., *The Origin of Races* (New York, 1963) though of general interest for human evolution also contains a bibliography and some chapters on Africa.

No general account of the origins of metallurgy in Africa has yet appeared.

On the Iron Age in East Africa, POSNANSKY, M., *Journal of African History*, vol. 2 (1961), pp. 177–99 contains references and gives a summary of the pottery sequence. Important accounts of single sites are LEAKEY, M. D., 'Report on the excavations at Hyrax Hill, Nakuru, Kenya Colony, 1937–38', *Trans. Royal Society of South Africa*, vol. 30 (1945), pp. 271–409; and LEAKEY, M. D. & L. S. B., *Excavations at the Njoro River Cave* (Oxford, 1950).

For the Azanian civilization myth, HUNTINGFORD, G. W. B., 'The Azanian Civilization of Kenya', *Antiquity*, vol. VII (1933), pp. 153–6: and GALLOWAY, A., 'Stone Structures on the Uasin Gishu Plateau', *South African Journal of Science*, vol. XXVII (1935), pp. 656–68, provide the foundation on which MURDOCK (1959) op. cit. and DAVIDSON (1959) *op. cit.* have amplified.

From outside East Africa the following are important:

NENQUIN, J., *Excavations at Sanga* (Musée Royal de l'Afrique Centrale, Brussels, 1957).

ROBINSON, K. R., *Khami Ruins* (Cambridge, 1959).

SUMMERS, R., *Inyanga* (Cambridge, 1958).

SUMMERS, R., & ROBINSON, K. R., *Zimbabwe Excavations* 1958. Occasional Papers No. 23A of the National Museums of Southern Rhodesia, 1963.

Part 3

THE HISTORY AND ARCHAEOLOGY OF
THE EAST AFRICAN COAST

General Books

AXELSON, E. *South-East Africa, 1488–1530* (London, 1940) (out of print).

The Portuguese in South-East Africa, 1600–1700 (Johannesburg, 1960).

DUYVENDAK, J. J. L. *China's discovery of Africa* (London, 1949). An account of the slight knowledge of East Africa possessed by the Chinese.

FREEMAN-GRENVILLE, G. S. P. 'Ibn Batuta's visit to East Africa, A.D. 1332', *Uganda Journal*, vol. 19 (1955), pp. 1–6.

East African Coast, Select Documents. From the first to the earlier nineteenth century (Oxford, 1962). An anthology of extracts from early writings on the Coast beginning with the *Periplus*, including the Arab travellers and early European visitors.

GROTTANELLI, V. L. *Pescatori del Oceano Indiano* (Rome, 1955). Concerns the modern coastal peoples of the Lamu–Kisimaiu region, but has an historical summary.

GUILLAIN, M.   *Documents sur l'histoire, la géographie et le commerce de l'Afrique orientale* (3 vols. and album) (Paris, 1856).

REUSCH, R.   *History of East Africa* (Stuttgart, 1954). Though defective in scholarship, documentation, and English this book is of greater value than has been allowed.

PRINS, A. H. J.   *The Swahili-Speaking Peoples of Zanzibar and the East African Coast.* Ethnographic Survey of Africa. (East Central Africa, XII) (London, International African Institute, 1961.)

SCHOFF, W. H.   *The Periplus of the Erythrean Sea.* Translation (New York). The earliest account by a Greek of the trade of the Indian Ocean, including East Africa, with valuable notes by Schoff on the commodities mentioned.

STRANDES, J.   *The Portuguese Period in East Africa*, translation by J. F. WALLWORK of *Die Portugiesenzeit von Deutsch und Englisch Ostafrika* (1899) with notes by J. S. KIRKMAN. Kenya History Society, Nairobi, 1961. The only work dealing with the whole Portuguese period. The notes incorporate the results of recent research.

Ceramics, coins, beads, etc.

The first three works provide excellent accounts of the most complete coastal excavations.

KIRKMAN, J. S.   *The Arab City of Gedi, Excavations at the Great Mosque* (Oxford, 1954). Contains the first and most exhaustive account of pottery found on the coast.
'The Tomb of the Dated Inscription at Gedi'. *Roy. Anthrop. Inst. Occ. Paper 14* (1960). Describes the most securely dated pottery, etc. from this important coastal town.
Gedi the Palace (The Hague, 1963).

FREEMAN-GRENVILLE, G. S. P.   'Coinage in East Africa before the Portuguese Times', *Numismatic Chron.*, vol. 17 (1957).
'East African Coin Finds', *Journal of African History*, vol. 1 (1960), pp. 31–43.

WALKER, J.   'History and Coinage of Sultans of Kilwa', *Numismatic Chrons.*, vol. XVI (1936) and see vol. XIX (1939); both republished with an added note by G. S. P. FREEMAN-GRENVILLE in *Tanganyika Notes and Records*, vol. 45, pp. 33–65.

Kenya

KIRKMAN, J. S.

'Historical Archaeology in Kenya, 1948–56', *Antiquaries Journal*, vol. 37, pp. 16–29.

'Great Pillars of Malindi and Mambrui', *Oriental Art*, vol. 4 (1958), 2.

Gedi. *Guide Brochure* (Mombasa, 1958).

Fort Jesus Guide (Mombasa, 1962).

KRAPF, J. L.

Travels, Researches and Missionary Labours during an eighteen years' residence in East Africa. (1 vol.) (London, 1860).

PRINS, A. H. J.

Coastal Tribes of the North-East Bantu (London International African Institute, 1952). Excellent account of the Nyika peoples of the coast of Kenya.

STIGAND, C. H.

Land of Zinj (London, 1913). Includes the longest version of the History of Pate.

Tanzania

CHITTICK, N.

Kisimani Mafia. Excavations at an Islamic Settlement on the East African coast. Occ. Paper 1. Department of Antiquities, Government Printer, Dar es Salaam (1962).

'Notes on Kilwa', *Tanganyika Notes and Records*, vol. 53 (1959), pp. 179–203, and *Guide to Kilwa* published periodically by Antiquities Division, Dar-es-Salaam.

'Kilwa and the Arab settlement of the East African coast', *Journal of African History*, vol. IV (1963), pp. 179–90, a further paper appeared in vol. VII, (1965).

FREEMAN-GRENVILLE, G. S. P.

'Some recent archaeological work on the Tanganyika Coast', *Man*, vol. 58 (1958), p. 155.

The Medieval History of the coast of Tanganyika, with special reference to recent archaeological discoveries. (Oxford, 1962). Largely devoted to an exhaustive analysis of the Kilwa Chronicle. The archaeological sections are defective and no reference is made to work later than March 1956.

Zanzibar and Pemba

GRAY, SIR JOHN   *History of Zanzibar from the Middle Ages to 1856* (Cambridge, 1962). Mainly concerned with the nineteenth century. Contains an excellent bibliography.

PEARCE, F. B.   *Zanzibar* (London, 1920). Old-fashioned but with some good descriptions of old sites.

Part 4

ORAL TRADITIONS AND THE REMEMBERED PAST
OF EAST AFRICA

VANSINA, J. *Oral Traditions* (London, 1964) is the only manual on the subject. The same author's two articles on 'Recording the Oral History of the Bakuba' in the *Journal of African History*, vol. I (1960) should also be consulted.

Surveys of the traditions of the Western Kingdoms of Uganda are contained in: OLIVER, R., 'The Traditional Histories of Buganda, Bunyoro and Ankole', *Journal of the Royal Anthropolotical Institute*, vol. 85 (1955), pp. 111–117 and POSNANSKY, M., 'Towards an Historical Geography of Uganda', *East African Geographical Review*, vol. 1 (1963), pp. 7–20.

FALLERS, MARGARET C., *The Eastern Lacustrine Bantu*, Part XI of the East Central African Ethnographic Survey or Africa (London, 1960), contains a survey of the literature in Luganda and on Buganda and Busoga whilst TAYLOR, BRIAN, *The Western Lacustrine Bantu* (1962) which is volume XIII in the same series, covers the literature on Ankole, Bunyoro and Buhaya.

SOUTHALL, A. W., 'Alur Tradition and its Historical significance', *Uganda Journal*, vol. 18 (1954), pp. 137–65, provides an anthropological account of a series of important traditions from the West Nile district of Uganda.

Important works in English on the history of different regions are:

CORY, H.   *History of Bukoba* (Mwanza, 1958).
    Sukuma Law and Custom (Oxford, 1953).
    The Ntemi (London, 1951).

CRAZZOLARA, J. P.   *The Lwoo*, 3 volumes (Verona, 1950–4). Invaluable on the Nilotic-speaking peoples.

DUNBAR, A.   *A History of Bunyoro* (Nairobi, 1965).

GULLIVER, P. J.   'The Karomojong Cluster', *Africa*, vol. XXII (1952). Gives an account of the traditions of some of the Nilo-Hamites. For regional ac-

G

counts see HAMILTON, R.A. (ed.), *History and Archaeology in Africa*, report of the 1953, London Conference (1955). The East African Literature Bureau publishes a catalogue of the more readily available sources in vernacular languages.

MORRIS, H. F.   *A History of Ankole* (Kampala, 1962).

OBERG, K.   'The Kingdom of Ankole' in *African Political Systems*, ed. M. Fortes and E. D. Evans-Pritchard (London, 1940), pp. 121–62.

RICHARDS, A. I. (ed.) *East African Chiefs: A study of political developments in some Uganda and Tanganyika tribes* (1960).

ROSCOE, J.   *The Baganda* (London, 1911) reprinted 1965.

WRIGLEY, C.   'Some thoughts on the Bacwezi', *Uganda Journal*, vol. 22 (1958), pp. 11–18.

Index

Abacwezi (Bacwezi), 9. 138, 157–8
Abraham, D. P., 122
Acheulean industry, 34–38, 41–42, 44–50
Acheuleo-Levalloisian (Fauresmith) culture, 44, 46
Acholi, 78, 145
Aden, Gulf of, 106, 109, 112
Adulis, 71, 110
age organizations, 77, 80
agriculture, origins and development of, 5, 49–50, 68, 69, 74, 77, 78–79, 80–86, 90–94, 101; Indonesian crops, 5; *see also* Cattle.
Agumba, 138
Akan-speaking peoples (W. Africa), 68
al-Hasan, Ali ibn (Sultan of Kilwa), 127
Al-Biruni, 113
Allbrook, D., 15
amakondere, trumpet-like instrument, 156–7
Amhara, Amharic speakers, 72, 116
Ankole, Banyankore, 138, 139
Arabs, Indian Ocean trade by, 5, 106; scholars, 58, 104; immigration into Africa, 69, 70–72, 110, 112, 123; influence in E. A. hinterland, 79–80, 88, 90, 104, 138, 143–4, 145; settlements along E. A. Coast, 106, 114, 119–21, 125
Arabic, inscriptions, 129; texts, records, 7, 111–114, 118, 127, 135; use of at Kilwa, 129
Architecture, at Kilwa, 127–30
Asia, appearance of handaxes late in, 2, 39; Mousterian and Levalloisian industries, 46, 47; microlithic industry in, 49; influences on Africa, 85, 87–88, 93; *see also* food crops
Asians, trade with Africa, 107
australopithecenes, 2, 21, 23–24, 27, 32, 33
Axelson, E., 122
Azania (E. A. coast), 109–10; 'Azanian civilization' (hinterland), 76, 95–96

Bacwezi, *see* Abacwezi
Bagamoyo, 117
Bantu languages, origin and dispersal, 5, 6, 72–75, 81, 90–93, 105, 106, 121
Bantu-speaking peoples, 5, 7, 63, 71–81, 82, 90, 138
Baraguyu, *see* Kwavi
Barawa (medieval coastal town in Somalia), 106, 114, 116, 119, 122

de Barros, Portuguese author, 123
baskets, basketry, 92
batemi (Sukuma rulers), 78
Bena, 79–80
Benadir (area of Somali coast), 106, 109, 121, 123
Bende (Tanzania people), 79
Benin, 67
Berbers, 69–70
Bey, Mirale, 119–20
Bigo earthworks, Uganda, 9
Birnin Kudu, Nigeria rock gong site, 56
Bishop, W. W., 2
blade and burin industries, 47–49
Bondei, 81
Boni (Kenya remnant people), 77
Bornu, 6, 69
Boskopoids, 62, 71, 76, 91
Brain, C. K., 27
brain size, in hominids, 34; in *Zinjanthropus*, 23; in *Homo habilis*, 31–32
Broken Hill, hominid site (*Homo Rhodesiensis*), 31, 47
Broom, R., 28
Buganda, Kingdom of, 9, 86, 138, 159–66; *Kabakas*, 86, 138, 159–62, 165–6
Bunyoro, Kingdom of, 78
Burton, R., prejudices about Africans, 143–4
Bushman, 52, 55, 61, 62, 71, 75, 76, 91, 105
Bwanjai, Tanzania rock painting sites, 52, 56
Bweranyange, capital of Karagwe Kingdom, 149, 154, 156–7

Cattle, 53, 58–59, 86–89, 92, 93, 98–99, 102; Social importance of in Karagwe, 157–8; Bantu and Nilotic words for, 164–5
caucasoid (human physical type), 62, 70–72, 76, 89, 92, 93
Chad, Lake, 83, 87, 90, 92
Chadic peoples (W. Africa), 68
Chagga, 76, 77
Chapman, S., 99
Chellean, Phase of Acheulean, 16, 27, 31, 34, 36, 44
Chemartin, Kenya excavation site, 102
Cherangani (Kenya mountain range), cairns at, 102–3
Childe, V. G., 142
China, trade with E. African coast, 113, 121, 132; documents, 113; *see also* porcelain